POCKET
CHEF

Beautiful
Bakes

igloobooks

igloobooks

Published in 2016
by Igloo Books Ltd
Cottage Farm
Sywell
NN6 0BJ
www.igloobooks.com

Food photography and recipe development:
© Stockfood, The Food Media Agency
Cover image © Marilyn Conway / Getty Images

LEO002 0716
2 4 6 8 10 9 7 5 3
ISBN 978-1-78557-537-2

Cover designed by Nicholas Gage
Interiors designed by Charles Wood-Penn
Edited by Caroline Icke

Printed and manufactured in China

Contents

Breads

Wholemeal Basil Bread

MAKES 1 LOAF

PREPARATION TIME 2 HOURS 30 MINUTES

COOKING TIME 35–40 MINUTES

INGREDIENTS

200 g / 7 oz / 1 ⅓ cups strong white bread flour, plus extra for dusting
200 g / 7 oz / 1 ⅓ cups stoneground wholemeal flour
½ tsp easy-blend dried yeast
1 tbsp caster (superfine) sugar
1 tsp fine sea salt
a small bunch of basil, chopped
3 tbsp olive oil

METHOD

1. Mix together the flours, yeast, sugar, salt and basil. Stir the oil into 280 ml / 9 fl. oz / 1 cup warm water, then mix with the dry ingredients.

2. Knead the mixture on a lightly oiled surface for 10 minutes or until smooth and elastic. Leave the dough to rest in an oiled bowl for 1–2 hours or until doubled in size.

3. Roll the dough with your hands into a fat sausage, then turn it 90° and roll it tightly the other way. Tuck the ends under and transfer the dough to a square or rectangular loaf tin, keeping the seam underneath. Cover the tin loosely with oiled cling film and leave to prove somewhere warm for 45 minutes.

4. Preheat the oven to 220°C (200°C fan) / 430F / gas 7.

5. Transfer the tin to the top shelf of the oven, then close the door. Bake for 35–40 minutes or until the loaf sounds hollow when you tap it underneath. Transfer the bread to a wire rack and leave to cool completely before slicing.

TOP TIP
Try replacing the basil with dill to make a great accompaniment to smoked salmon.

Sesame Rolls

MAKES 12 ROLLS

PREPARATION TIME 2 HOURS 30 MINUTES

COOKING TIME 15 MINUTES

INGREDIENTS

400 g / 14 oz / 2 ⅔ cups strong white bread flour,
  plus extra for dusting

1 tsp easy-blend dried yeast

1 bsp caster (superfine) sugar

1 tsp fine sea salt

1 bsp sesame oil

1 bsp sesame seeds

METHOD

1. Mix together the flour, yeast, sugar and salt. Stir the oil into 280 ml / 9 fl. oz / 1 cup of warm water, then stir it into the dry ingredients.

2. Knead the mixture on a lightly oiled surface for 10 minutes or until smooth and elastic. Leave the dough to rest, covered with oiled cling film, for 1–2 hours or until doubled in size.

3. Shape the dough into 12 rolls and transfer to a greased baking tray, then cover with oiled cling film and leave to prove for 1 hour or until doubled in size.

4. Preheat the oven to 220°C (200°C fan) / 425F / gas 7.

5. Slash a cross into the top of each roll with a sharp knife and sprinkle with sesame seeds. Transfer the tray to the top shelf of the oven, then close the door.

6. Bake for 15 minutes or until the rolls sound hollow when you tap them underneath. Transfer to a wire rack and leave to cool completely before serving.

TOP TIP

Try filling the rolls with hummus and slices of chargrilled lamb.

Rice Bread

MAKES 1 LOAF

PREPARATION TIME 2 HOURS 30 MINUTES

COOKING TIME 35–40 MINUTES

INGREDIENTS

300 g / 10 ½ oz / 2 cups strong white bread flour,
    plus extra for dusting
½ tsp easy-blend dried yeast
1 tbsp caster (superfine) sugar
1 tsp fine sea salt
300 g / 10 ½ oz / 1 ¾ cups cooked white rice,
    cooled
1 tbsp olive oil

METHOD

1. Mix together the flour, yeast, sugar and
   salt. Stir the rice and oil into 280 ml /
   9 fl. oz / 1 cup of warm water and mix with
   the dry ingredients.

2. Knead the dough on a lightly oiled surface
   for 10 minutes or until smooth and elastic.
   Leave the dough to rest, covered with oiled
   cling film, for 1–2 hours or until doubled
   in size.

3. Roll the dough into a fat sausage, then
   turn it 90° and roll it tightly the other way.
   Tuck the ends under and transfer the dough
   to a greased loaf tin, making sure to keep
   the seam underneath.

4. Cover the tin and leave to prove for 1 hour
   or until doubled in size.

5. Meanwhile, preheat the oven to 220°C
   (200°C fan) / 430F / gas 7.

6. Bake for 35–40 minutes or until the loaf
   sounds hollow when you tap it underneath.
   Transfer the bread to a wire rack and leave
   to cool completely before slicing.

TOP TIP

Try using the bread
to make coronation
chicken sandwiches.

ogurt Bread

KES **2 LOAVES**

PARATION TIME **2 HOURS 30 MINUTES**

KING TIME **30 MINUTES**

GREDIENTS

g / 10 ½ oz / 2 cups strong white bread flour,
lus extra for dusting
p easy-blend dried yeast
sp caster (superfine) sugar
o fine sea salt
ml / 10 ½ fl. oz / 1 ¼ cups natural yogurt,
lus extra for brushing

METHOD

1. Mix together the flour, yeast, sugar and salt,
   then stir in the yogurt.

2. Knead the dough on a lightly oiled surface
   for 10 minutes or until smooth and elastic.
   Leave the dough to rest, covered with oiled
   cling film, for 1–2 hours or until doubled
   in size.

3. Divide the dough in half and shape each
   piece into a square loaf. Transfer to a
   greased baking tray, cover with oiled cling
   film and leave to prove for 1 hour or until
   doubled in size.

4. Meanwhile, preheat the oven to 220°C
   (200°C fan) / 430F / gas 7.

5. Brush the top of the loaves with yogurt or
   leave them plain. Bake for 30 minutes or
   until the loaves sound hollow when you tap
   them underneath. Transfer to a wire rack
   and leave to cool completely.

TOP TIP

Try adding the grated
zest of a lemon to
the dough for a
fragrant bread.

15

Granary and Rye Batons

MAKES 8 BATONS

PREPARATION TIME 2 HOURS 30 MINUTES

COOKING TIME 20 MINUTES

INGREDIENTS

200 g / 7 oz / 1 ⅓ cups malted granary flour
200 g / 7 oz / 1 ⅓ cups rye flour
1 tsp easy-blend dried yeast
2 tbsp caster (superfine) sugar
2 tbsp poppy seeds
1 tsp fine sea salt
1 tbsp olive oil

METHOD

1. Mix together the flours, yeast, sugar, poppy seeds and salt. Stir the oil into 280 / 9 fl. oz / 1 cup of warm water, then stir into the dry ingredients.

2. Knead the mixture on a lightly oiled surf for 10 minutes or until smooth and elast Leave the dough to rest in a lightly oiled bowl, covered with oiled cling film, for 1–2 hours or until doubled in size.

3. Knead it for 2 more minutes, then divide it into 8 pieces and shape into slender batons. Transfer the batons to a greased baking tray and cover with oiled cling film Leave to prove for 1 hour or until doubled in size.

4. Meanwhile, preheat the oven to 220°C (200°C fan) / 425F / gas 7.

5. Transfer the tray to the top shelf of the oven. Bake for 20 minutes or until the batons sound hollow when you tap them underneath. Transfer to a wire rack and leave to cool completely.

TOP TIP
These batons taste great filled with smoked salmon and cream cheese.

Cranberry and Flaked Almond Loaf

MAKES **1 LOAF**

PREPARATION TIME **15 MINUTES**

COOKING TIME **55 MINUTES**

INGREDIENTS

225 g / 8 oz / 1 ½ cups self-raising flour
100 g / 3 ½ oz / ½ cup butter, cubed
75 g / 3 oz / ⅓ cup caster (superfine) sugar
150 g / 5 ½ oz / ¾ cup dried cranberries
75 g / 2 ½ oz / 1 cup flaked (slivered) almonds
1 large egg
75 ml / 2 ½ fl. oz / ⅓ cup whole milk

METHOD

1. Preheat the oven to 180°C (160°C fan) / 355F / gas 4 and line a loaf tin with greaseproof paper.

2. Sieve the flour into a mixing bowl and rub in the butter until it resembles fine breadcrumbs, then stir in the sugar, cranberries and almonds.

3. Lightly beat the egg with the milk and stir it into the dry ingredients until just combined.

4. Scrape the mixture into the loaf tin and bake for 55 minutes or until a skewer inserted into the centre comes out clean.

5. Transfer the cake to a wire rack and leave to cool completely.

TOP TIP

Try replacing the cranberries with dried sour cherries.

White Bread Rolls

MAKES **12 ROLLS**

PREPARATION TIME **2 HOURS 15 MINUTES**

COOKING TIME **15 MINUTES**

INGREDIENTS

400 g / 14 oz / 2 ⅔ cups strong white bread flour,
    plus extra for dusting
½ tsp easy-blend dried yeast
1 tbsp caster (superfine) sugar
1 tsp fine sea salt
1 tbsp olive oil

METHOD

1. Mix together the flour, yeast, sugar and salt. Stir the oil into 280 ml / 9 fl. oz / 1 cup of warm water, then stir it into the dry ingredients.

2. Knead the mixture on a lightly oiled surfac for 10 minutes or until smooth and elastic. Leave the dough to rest, covered with oile cling film, for 1–2 hours or until doubled in size.

3. Shape the dough into 12 rolls and transfer to a greased baking tray, then cover with oiled cling film and leave to prove for 1 hou or until doubled in size.

4. Preheat the oven to 220°C (200°C fan) / 425F / gas 7.

5. Dust the rolls with a little flour and slash a cross into the top of each one with a shar knife. Transfer the tray to the top shelf of t oven, then close the door.

6. Bake for 15 minutes or until the rolls soun hollow when you tap them underneath. Transfer to a wire rack and leave to cool completely before serving.

TOP TIP

Freeze any leftover rolls on the day of baking and defrost in a hot oven for 10 minutes.

nion
ocaccia

MAKES **1 FOCACCIA**

PREPARATION TIME **2 HOURS 30 MINUTES**

COOKING TIME **25 MINUTES**

INGREDIENTS

0 g / 10 ½ oz / 2 cups strong white bread flour

sp easy-blend dried yeast

sp fine sea salt

bsp olive oil

nion, quartered and thinly sliced

bsp thyme leaves

ml / 1 ¾ fl. oz / ¼ cup olive oil

ml / 1 ¾ fl. oz / ¼ cup warm water

sp fine sea salt

METHOD

1. Mix together the flour, yeast and salt. Stir the oil into 280 ml / 9 fl. oz / 1 cup of warm water, then stir it into the dry ingredients.

2. Knead the mixture on a lightly oiled surface for 10 minutes or until smooth and elastic. Leave the dough to rest, covered with oiled cling film, for 1–2 hours or until doubled in size.

3. Oil a rectangular cake tin, then stretch out the dough to cover the base. Cover the focaccia with oiled cling film and leave to prove for 1 hour or until doubled in size.

4. Preheat the oven to 220°C (200°C fan) / 430F / gas 7.

5. Sprinkle the onion and thyme over the top of the focaccia and press down lightly. Combine the oil, water and salt in a jar and shake well. Pour it all over the dough.

6. Transfer the tin to the top shelf of the oven. Bake for 25 minutes or until the top is golden and the base is cooked through. Leave to cool on a wire rack before cutting into squares.

TOP TIP

Dot the top of the focaccia with pieces of salted anchovy before baking.

Sweetcorn Rolls

MAKES 16 ROLLS

PREPARATION TIME 2 HOURS 30 MINUTES

COOKING TIME 15 MINUTES

INGREDIENTS

400 g / 14 oz / 2 ⅔ cups strong white bread flour, plus extra for dusting

½ tsp easy-blend dried yeast

1 tbsp caster (superfine) sugar

1 tsp fine sea salt

1 tbsp olive oil

100 g / 3 ½ oz / ½ cup canned sweetcorn, drained

METHOD

1. Mix together the flour, yeast, sugar and salt. Stir the oil and sweetcorn into 280 ml / 9 fl. oz / 1 cup of warm water, then stir it into the dry ingredients.

2. Knead the mixture on a lightly oiled surface for 10 minutes or until smooth and elastic. Leave the dough to rest in a lightly oiled bowl, covered with oiled cling film, for 1–2 hours or until doubled in size.

3. Knead the dough for 2 more minutes, then split it into 16 even pieces and shape into rolls. Transfer the rolls to a greased baking tray and cover with oiled cling film. Leave to prove for 1 hour or until doubled in size.

4. Meanwhile, preheat the oven to 220°C (200°C fan) / 425F / gas 7.

5. Transfer the tray to the top shelf of the oven, then close the door. Bake for 15 minutes or until the rolls sound hollow when you tap them underneath. Transfer to a wire rack and leave to cool completely.

TOP TIP

Try filling the rolls with spicy chicken and slices of avocado.

Black Olive and Feta Bread

MAKES 1 LOAF

PREPARATION TIME 2 HOURS 30 MINUTES

COOKING TIME 35–40 MINUTES

INGREDIENTS

300 g / 10 ½ oz / 2 cups strong white bread flour,
  plus extra for dusting

100 g / 3 ½ oz / ⅔ cup stoneground
  wholemeal flour

1 tsp easy-blend dried yeast

1 tbsp caster (superfine) sugar

1 tsp fine sea salt

100 g / 3 ½ oz / ½ cup feta, cubed

100 g / 3 ½ oz / ½ cup black olives,
  pitted and sliced

METHOD

1. Mix together the flours, yeast, sugar and salt. Stir the feta and olives into 280 ml / 9 fl. oz / 1 cup of warm water and stir into the dry ingredients.

2. Knead the mixture on a lightly oiled surface for 10 minutes or until the dough is smooth and elastic. Leave the dough to rest in a lightly oiled bowl, covered with oiled cling film, for 1–2 hours or until doubled in size.

3. Knead the dough for 2 more minutes, then roll it into a fat sausage. Turn it 90° and roll it tightly the other way, then tuck the ends under and transfer the dough to the tin, keeping the seam underneath.

4. Cover the tin with oiled cling film and leave to prove for 45 minutes.

5. Preheat the oven to 220°C (200°C fan) / 430F / gas 7.

6. Transfer the tin to the top shelf of the oven, then close the door. Bake for 35–40 minutes or until the underneath sounds hollow when tapped. Leave to cool completely on a wire rack before slicing.

TOP TIP
This bread also tastes great made with goats' cheese in place of the feta.

27

Crusty Lemon Rolls

MAKES 4 ROLLS

PREPARATION TIME 2 HOURS 30 MINUTES

COOKING TIME 20 MINUTES

INGREDIENTS

400 g / 14 oz / 2 ⅔ cups strong white bread flour,
    plus extra for dusting
½ tsp easy-blend dried yeast
1 tbsp caster (superfine) sugar
1 tsp fine sea salt
1 lemon, juiced and zest finely grated
1 tbsp olive oil

METHOD

1. Mix together the flour, yeast, sugar, salt a
   lemon zest. Stir the oil and lemon juice in
   250 ml / 9 fl. oz / 1 cup of warm water, the
   stir it into the dry ingredients.

2. Knead the mixture on a lightly oiled surfa
   for 10 minutes or until smooth and elastic
   Leave the dough to rest, covered with oile
   cling film, for 1–2 hours or until doubled
   in size.

3. Shape into 4 long rolls and transfer to a
   greased baking tray, then cover with oiled
   cling film and leave to prove for 1 hour or
   until doubled in size.

4. Preheat the oven to 220°C (200°C fan)
   / 425F / gas 7.

5. Slash the top of each roll diagonally with
   a sharp knife. Transfer the tray to the top
   shelf of the oven, then close the door.

6. Bake for 20 minutes or until the rolls
   sound hollow when you tap them
   underneath. Transfer to a wire rack and
   leave to cool completely before serving.

TOP TIP

These rolls taste great filled with crumbled feta and sun-blush tomatoes.

loured Cob

MAKES 1 LOAF

PREPARATION TIME 2 HOURS 30 MINUTES

COOKING TIME 40 MINUTES

INGREDIENTS

- g / 14 oz / 2 ⅔ cups strong white bread flour, plus extra for dusting
- sp easy-blend dried yeast
- sp caster (superfine) sugar
- p fine sea salt
- sp olive oil

METHOD

1. Mix together the flour, yeast, sugar and salt. Stir the oil into 280 ml / 9 fl. oz / 1 cup of warm water, then stir it into the dry ingredients.

2. Knead the mixture on a lightly oiled surface for 10 minutes or until smooth and elastic. Leave the dough to rest, covered with oiled cling film, for 1–2 hours or until doubled in size.

3. Shape the dough into a round cob loaf and transfer to a greased baking tray, then cover with oiled cling film and leave to prove for 1 hour or until doubled in size.

4. Preheat the oven to 220°C (200°C fan) / 425F / gas 7.

5. Dust the loaf with flour. Transfer the tray to the top shelf of the oven, then close the door. Bake for 40 minutes or until the loaf sounds hollow when you tap it underneath. Transfer to a wire rack and leave to cool completely before serving.

TOP TIP

Hollow out the loaf and pack it full of mixed antipasti to make a picnic loaf.

Grape and Rosemary Focaccia

MAKES **1 FOCACCIA**

PREPARATION TIME **2 HOURS 30 MINUTES**

COOKING TIME **25 MINUTES**

INGREDIENTS

300 g / 10 ½ oz / 2 cups strong white bread flour
½ tsp easy-blend dried yeast
1 tsp fine sea salt
2 tbsp olive oil
75 g / 2 ½ oz / ½ cup seedless red grapes
1 tbsp rosemary
50 ml / 1 ¾ fl. oz / ¼ cup olive oil
50 ml / 1 ¾ fl. oz / ¼ cup warm water
½ tsp sea salt crystals

METHOD

1. Mix together the flour, yeast and salt. Stir the oil into 280 ml / 9 fl. oz / 1 cup of warm water then stir it into the dry ingredients.

2. Knead the mixture on a lightly oiled surface for 10 minutes or until smooth and elastic. Leave the dough to rest, covered with oiled cling film, for 1–2 hours or until doubled in size.

3. Oil a baking tray, then roll or stretch out the dough to a large oval. Place on the tray, cover with oiled cling film and leave to prove for 1 hour or until doubled in size.

4. Preheat the oven to 220°C (200°C fan) / 430F / gas 7.

5. Sprinkle the grapes and rosemary over the top of the focaccia and press down lightly. Combine the oil, water and salt in a jar and shake well. Pour it all over the dough.

6. Transfer the tin to the top shelf of the oven then close the door. Bake for 25 minutes or until the top is golden and the base is cooked through. Leave to cool on a wire rack before cutting into squares.

TOP TIP
Try replacing the rosemary with lavender flowers for an aromatic loaf.

Rosemary Focaccia

KES 1 FOCACCIA

EPARATION TIME 2 HOURS 30 MINUTES

OKING TIME 25 MINUTES

GREDIENTS

g / 10 ½ oz / 2 cups strong white bread flour
sp easy-blend dried yeast
p fine sea salt
sp olive oil
ml / 1 ¾ fl. oz / ¼ cup olive oil
ml / 1 ¾ fl. oz / ¼ cup warm water
sp fine sea salt
p dried rosemary

METHOD

1. Mix together the flour, yeast and salt. Stir the oil into 280 ml / 9 fl. oz / 1 cup of warm water then stir it into the dry ingredients.

2. Knead the mixture on a lightly oiled surface for 10 minutes or until smooth and elastic. Leave the dough to rest, covered with oiled cling film, for 1–2 hours or until doubled in size.

3. Oil a baking tray, then roll or stretch out the dough to a large oval. Place on the tray.

4. Cover the focaccia with oiled cling film and leave to prove for 1 hour or until doubled in size.

5. Preheat the oven to 220°C (200°C fan) / 430F / gas 7.

6. Combine the oil, water and salt in a jar and shake well. Pour it all over the dough, then sprinkle with the rosemary. Transfer the tin to the top shelf of the oven.

7. Bake for 25 minutes, then leave to cool on a wire rack before cutting into squares.

TOP TIP

Try replacing the rosemary with sprigs of fresh thyme.

Tear and Share Rolls

MAKES 9 ROLLS

PREPARATION TIME 2 HOURS 30 MINUTES

COOKING TIME 25 MINUTES

INGREDIENTS

400 g / 14 oz / 2 ⅔ cups strong white bread flour,
    plus extra for dusting
½ tsp easy-blend dried yeast
1 tbsp caster (superfine) sugar
1 tsp fine sea salt
1 tbsp olive oil

METHOD

1. Mix together the flour, yeast, sugar and salt. Stir the oil into 280 ml / 9 fl. oz / 1 cup of warm water then stir it into the dry ingredients.

2. Knead the mixture on a lightly oiled surface for 10 minutes or until smooth and elastic. Leave the dough to rest, covered with oiled cling film, for 1–2 hours or until doubled in size.

3. Shape the dough into 9 rolls and transfer to a greased cast iron sauté pan or large round cake tin. Cover with oiled cling film and prove for 1 hour or until doubled in size and the rolls are all touching.

4. Preheat the oven to 220°C (200°C fan) / 425F / gas 7.

5. Slash a cross into the top of each roll with a sharp knife. Transfer the tray to the top shelf of the oven, then close the door.

6. Bake for 25 minutes until the rolls sound hollow when you tap them underneath. Transfer to a wire rack and leave to cool completely before serving.

TOP TIP

Double the mixture and bake in a large roasting tin when you have lots of guests.

innamon and aisin Bread

KES 1 LOAF

PARATION TIME 2 HOURS 30 MINUTES

KING TIME 35–40 MINUTES

GREDIENTS

g / 14 oz / 2 ⅔ cups strong white bread flour,
lus extra for dusting

p easy-blend dried yeast

sp caster (superfine) sugar

ground cinnamon

fine sea salt

g / 3 ½ oz / ½ cup raisins

sp butter, melted

g, beaten

METHOD

1. Mix together the flour, yeast, sugar, cinnamon, salt and raisins. Stir the butter into 280 ml / 9 fl. oz / 1 cup of warm water. Stir the liquid into the dry ingredients, then knead on a lightly oiled surface for 10 minutes or until the dough is smooth and elastic.

2. Leave the dough to rest, covered with oiled cling film, for 1–2 hours or until doubled in size.

3. Knead the dough for 2 more minutes, then shape it into a long loaf. Transfer the dough to a greased loaf tin and cover again with oiled cling film. Leave to prove for 1 hour or until doubled in size.

4. Meanwhile, preheat the oven to 220°C (200°C fan) / 425F / gas 7.

5. When the dough has risen, brush the top with beaten egg and score a diamond pattern across the top. Transfer the tin to the top shelf of the oven close the door. Bake for 35–40 minutes or until the loaf is golden and sounds hollow when tapped.

TOP TIP
This bread makes excellent French toast.

Seed-topped Square Rolls

MAKES 9 ROLLS

PREPARATION TIME 2 HOURS 12 MINUTES

COOKING TIME 12 MINUTES

INGREDIENTS

400 g / 14 oz / 2 ⅔ cups strong white bread flour,
    plus extra for dusting
½ tsp easy-blend dried yeast
1 tbsp caster (superfine) sugar
1 tsp fine sea salt
2 tbsp olive oil
2 tbsp milk
sesame seeds, poppy seeds and linseeds
    for sprinkling

METHOD

1. Mix together the flour, yeast, sugar and s
   Stir the oil into 280 ml / 9 fl. oz / 1 cup of
   warm water, then stir the liquid into the
   dry ingredients.

2. Knead the mixture on a lightly oiled surfa
   for 10 minutes or until smooth and elasti
   Leave the dough to rest, covered with oil
   cling film, for 1–2 hours or until doubled
   in size.

3. Roll out the dough into a square, then cut
   into 9 rolls and transfer to a greased bak
   tray. Cover the rolls with oiled cling film
   leave to prove for 1 hour or until doubled
   in size.

4. Preheat the oven to 220°C (200°C fan)
   / 430F / gas 7.

5. Brush the rolls with milk and sprinkle the
   tops with your choice of seeds. Transfer t
   the top shelf of the oven, then close the d
   Bake for 12 minutes or until the rolls sou
   hollow when you tap them underneath.

TOP TIP

Try filling the rolls with a layer of smooth pâté for a picnic treat.

heese and acon Bread

KES 1 LOAF

PARATION TIME 2 HOURS 30 MINUTES

KING TIME 35 MINUTES

GREDIENTS

g / 14 oz / 2 ⅔ cups strong white bread flour, plus extra for dusting

sp easy-blend dried yeast

sp caster (superfine) sugar

p fine sea salt

g / 3 ½ oz / 1 cup streaky bacon, chopped

g / 3 ½ oz / 1 cup Cheddar, grated

nall bunch of chives, chopped

METHOD

1. Mix together the flour, yeast, sugar and salt. Stir the bacon, Cheddar cheese and chives into 280 ml / 9 fl. oz / 1 cup of warm water and stir into the dry ingredients.

2. Knead the mixture on a lightly oiled surface for 10 minutes or until the dough is smooth and elastic. Leave the dough to rest in a lightly oiled bowl, covered with oiled cling film, for 1–2 hours or until doubled in size.

3. Knead the dough for 2 more minutes, then roll it into a fat sausage. Turn it 90° and roll it tightly the other way, then tuck the ends under and transfer the dough to a lined baking tray, keeping the seam underneath.

4. Cover the dough loosely with oiled cling film and leave to prove for 45 minutes.

5. Preheat the oven to 220°C (200°C fan) / 430F / gas 7.

6. Transfer the tray to the top shelf of the oven. Bake for 35 minutes or until the underneath sounds hollow when tapped. Leave to cool completely on a wire rack before slicing.

TOP TIP
Serve the bread warm, spread with soft goats' cheese.

Rye Bread

MAKES 1 LOAF

PREPARATION TIME 2 HOURS 35 MINUTES

COOKING TIME 35–40 MINUTES

INGREDIENTS

400 g / 14 oz / 2 ⅔ cups rye flour, plus extra
    for dusting
1 tsp easy-blend dried yeast
1 tbsp treacle
1 tbsp malt extract
1 tsp fine sea salt
1 tbsp olive oil

METHOD

1. Mix together the flour, yeast, treacle, malt
   extract and salt. Stir the oil into 280 ml /
   9 fl. oz / 1 cup of warm water.

2. Stir the liquid into the dry ingredients,
   then knead on a lightly oiled surface for
   10 minutes or until the dough is smooth
   and elastic.

3. Leave the dough to rest, covered with oiled
   cling film, for 1–2 hours or until doubled in
   size. Knead the dough for 2 more minutes,
   then shape it into a round loaf.

4. Transfer the loaf to a greased baking tray
   and cover again with oiled cling film. Leave
   to prove for 1 hour or until doubled in size.

5. Meanwhile, preheat the oven to 220°C
   (200°C fan) / 430F / gas 7. When the dough
   has risen, dust the top with flour.

6. Transfer the tray to the top shelf of the oven,
   close the door. Bake for 35–40 minutes or
   until the loaf sounds hollow when tapped.
   Transfer the bread to a wire rack and leave
   to cool.

TOP TIP
This bread is great for
making pastrami
sandwiches.

eed-topped Vholemeal Rolls

KES 9 ROLLS

PARATION TIME 2 HOURS 30 MINUTES

KING TIME 12 MINUTES

GREDIENTS

g / 7 oz / 1 ⅓ cups strong white bread flour,
lus extra for dusting

g / 7 oz / 1 ⅓ cups stoneground
vholemeal flour

p easy-blend dried yeast

sp caster (superfine) sugar

o fine sea salt

sp olive oil

sp milk

ame seeds, poppy seeds and linseeds
or sprinkling

METHOD

1. Mix together the flours, yeast, sugar and salt. Stir the oil into 280 ml / 9 fl. oz / 1 cup of warm water, then stir the liquid into the dry ingredients.

2. Knead the mixture on a lightly oiled surface for 10 minutes or until smooth and elastic. Leave the dough to rest, covered with oiled cling film, for 1–2 hours or until doubled in size.

3. Roll out the dough into a square, then cut it into 9 rolls and transfer to a greased baking tray. Cover the rolls with oiled cling film and leave to prove for 1 hour or until doubled in size.

4. Preheat the oven to 220°C (200°C fan) / 430F / gas 7.

5. Brush the rolls with milk and sprinkle the tops with your choice of seeds. Transfer the tray to the top shelf of the oven, then close the door. Bake for 12 minutes or until the rolls sound hollow when you tap them underneath.

TOP TIP
These rolls are delicious filled with crab mayonnaise.

Baguettes

MAKES 2 BAGUETTES

PREPARATION TIME 2 HOURS 30 MINUTES

COOKING TIME 25 MINUTES

INGREDIENTS

350 g / 12 ½ oz / 1 ½ cups strong white bread
flour, plus extra for dusting
50 g / 1 ¾ oz / ⅓ cup stoneground
wholemeal flour
½ tsp easy-blend dried yeast
1 tbsp caster (superfine) sugar
1 tsp fine sea salt
1 tbsp olive oil

METHOD

1. Mix together the flours, yeast, sugar and
   salt. Stir the oil into 280 ml / 9 fl. oz / 1 cu
   of warm water, then stir it into the dry
   ingredients.

2. Knead the mixture on a lightly oiled surfa
   for 10 minutes or until smooth and elasti
   Leave the dough to rest, covered with oil
   cling film, for 1–2 hours or until doubled
   in size.

3. Roll the dough into a long baguette, then
   make a diagonal cut half way down to for
   2 shorter baguettes. Transfer the baguet
   to a greased baking tray, then cover with
   oiled cling film and leave to prove for
   1 hour or until doubled in size.

4. Preheat the oven to 220°C (200°C fan)
   / 425F / gas 7.

5. Dust the baguettes with a little flour and
   make a few diagonal slashes along the to
   with a sharp knife. Transfer the tray to th
   top shelf of the oven.

6. Bake for 25 minutes or until the baguette
   sound hollow when you tap them
   underneath. Transfer to a wire rack and
   leave to cool completely before serving.

TOP TIP
Serve for breakfast with unsalted butter and good strawberry jam (jelly).

Wholemeal Granary Batons

MAKES 6 BATONS

PREPARATION TIME 2 HOURS 30 MINUTES

BAKING TIME 20 MINUTES

INGREDIENTS

200 g / 7 oz / 1 ⅓ cups malted granary flour

200 g / 7 oz / 1 ⅓ cups wholemeal flour

7 g easy-blend dried yeast

1 tsp caster (superfine) sugar

1 tsp fine sea salt

1 tbsp olive oil

METHOD

1. Mix together the flours, yeast, sugar and salt. Stir the oil into 280 ml / 9 fl. oz / 1 cup of warm water, then stir it into the dry ingredients.

2. Knead the mixture on a lightly oiled surface with your hands for 10 minutes or until smooth and elastic. Leave the dough to rest in a lightly oiled bowl, covered with oiled cling film, for 1–2 hours or until doubled in size.

3. Knead it for 2 more minutes, then divide it into 6 pieces and shape into even batons. Transfer the batons to a greased baking tray and cover with oiled cling film. Leave to prove for 1 hour or until doubled in size.

4. Meanwhile, preheat the oven to 220°C (200°C fan) / 425F / gas 7.

5. Slash the tops of the batons with a sharp knife. Transfer the tray to the top shelf of the oven, then close the door. Bake for 20 minutes or until the batons sound hollow when you tap them underneath. Transfer to a wire rack and leave to cool completely.

TOP TIP

Try filling the batons with home-cooked ham and grain mustard mayonnaise.

Crusty Walnut Rolls

MAKES **12 ROLLS**

PREPARATION TIME **2 HOURS 30 MINUTES**

COOKING TIME **12 MINUTES**

INGREDIENTS

200 g / 7 oz / 1 ⅓ cups strong white bread flour,
    plus extra for dusting
200 g / 7 oz / 1 ⅓ cups stoneground wholemeal
    flour
½ tsp easy-blend dried yeast
1 tbsp caster (superfine) sugar
75 g / 2 ½ oz / ⅔ cup walnuts, chopped
1 tsp fine sea salt
2 tbsp olive oil

METHOD

1. Mix together the flours, yeast, sugar,
   walnuts and salt. Stir the oil into 280 ml
   / 9 fl. oz / 1 cup of warm water, then stir
   the liquid into the dry ingredients.

2. Knead the mixture on a lightly oiled surfa
   for 10 minutes or until smooth and elasti
   Leave the dough to rest, covered with oile
   cling film, for 1–2 hours or until doubled
   in size.

3. Roll out the dough into a square, then cut
   it into 12 rectangular rolls and transfer t
   a greased baking tray. Cover the rolls wit
   oiled cling film and leave to prove for 1 h
   or until doubled in size.

4. Preheat the oven to 220°C (200°C fan)
   / 430F / gas 7.

5. Transfer the tray to the top shelf of the ov
   then close the door. Bake for 12 minutes
   until the rolls sound hollow when you tap
   them underneath.

TOP TIP
Try filling the rolls
with blue cheese and
pickled pears.

Long-ferment Bread

MAKES 1 LOAF

PREPARATION TIME 14 HOURS 30 MINUTES

BAKING TIME 45 MINUTES

INGREDIENTS

200 g / 7 oz / 1 ⅓ cups strong white bread flour

200 g / 7 oz / 1 ⅓ cups wholemeal flour

1 tbsp rye flour

1 tbsp easy-blend dried yeast

1 tbsp caster (superfine) sugar

1 tbsp fine sea salt

2 tbsp olive oil

METHOD

1. Mix together the flours, yeast, sugar and salt. Stir the oil into 280 ml / 9 fl. oz / 1 cup of warm water then stir it into the dry ingredients.

2. Knead the mixture on a lightly oiled surface with your hands for 10 minutes or until smooth and elastic. Put the dough in a lightly oiled bowl, covered with oiled cling film, then put in the fridge for 6 hours or until doubled in size.

3. Knead it for 2 more minutes, then shape it into a round loaf. Transfer the loaf to a greased baking tray and cover with oiled cling film. Return to the fridge and leave to prove for 6 hours. Remove from the fridge and leave to come up to temperature and finish rising for 1–2 hours or until doubled in size.

4. Meanwhile, preheat the oven to 220°C (200°C fan) / 425F / gas 7.

5. Slash the top with a sharp knife. Transfer the tray to the top shelf of the oven, then close the door. Bake for 45 minutes or until the loaf sounds hollow when you tap it underneath. Transfer to a wire rack and leave to cool completely.

TOP TIP

This bread makes really good toast up to 5 days after baking.

Seeded White Rolls

MAKES 8 ROLLS

PREPARATION TIME 2 HOURS 30 MINUTES

COOKING TIME 12 MINUTES

INGREDIENTS

400 g / 14 oz / 2 ⅔ cups strong white bread flour,
plus extra for dusting
2 tbsp sunflower seeds
2 tbsp linseeds
1 tbsp pumpkin seeds
½ tsp easy-blend dried yeast
1 tbsp caster (superfine) sugar
1 tsp fine sea salt
1 tbsp olive oil

METHOD

1. Mix together the flour, seeds, yeast, sugar
   and salt. Stir the oil into 280 ml / 9 fl. oz /
   1 cup of warm water then stir the liquid
   into the dry ingredients.

2. Knead the mixture on a lightly oiled surface
   for 10 minutes or until smooth and elastic.
   Leave the dough to rest, covered with oiled
   cling film, for 1–2 hours or until doubled
   in size.

3. Divide the dough into 8 evenly-sized pieces
   and shape into rolls on a greased baking
   tray. Cover the rolls with oiled cling film
   and leave to prove for 1 hour or until
   doubled in size.

4. Preheat the oven to 220°C (200°C fan)
   / 430F / gas 7.

5. Transfer the tray to the top shelf of the
   oven, close the door. Bake for 12 minutes
   or until the rolls sound hollow when you
   tap them underneath. Transfer the rolls
   to a wire rack and leave to cool completely.

TOP TIP

These rolls taste great filled with tuna mayonnaise and sliced cucumber.

ustic ocaccia

KES 1 FOCACCIA

EPARATION TIME 2 HOURS 30 MINUTES

)KING TIME 25 MINUTES

GREDIENTS

g / 10 ½ oz / 2 cups strong white bread flour
sp easy-blend dried yeast
p fine sea salt
sp olive oil

METHOD

1. Mix together the flour, yeast and salt. Stir the oil into 280 ml / 9 fl. oz / 1 cup of warm water then stir it into the dry ingredients.

2. Knead the mixture on a lightly oiled surface for 10 minutes or until smooth and elastic. Leave the dough to rest, covered with oiled cling film, for 1–2 hours or until doubled in size.

3. Oil a rectangular cake tin, then stretch out the dough to cover the base. Cover the focaccia with oiled cling film and leave to prove for 1 hour or until doubled in size.

4. Preheat the oven to 220°C (200°C fan) / 430F / gas 7.

5. Transfer the tin to the top shelf of the oven, then close the door. Bake for 25 minutes or until the top is golden and the base is cooked through. Leave to cool completely on a wire rack.

TOP TIP
Serve the focaccia with a bowl of pesto for dipping.

Cheese Fougasse

MAKES 2 LOAVES

PREPARATION TIME 2 HOURS 30 MINUTES

COOKING TIME 25 MINUTES

INGREDIENTS

400 g / 14 oz / 2 ⅔ cups strong white bread flour,
    plus extra for dusting
½ tsp easy-blend dried yeast
4 tbsp Parmesan, finely grated
1 tsp fine sea salt
3 tbsp olive oil, plus extra for brushing
150 g / 5 ½ oz / 1 ½ cups Gruyère, grated

METHOD

1. Mix together the flours, yeast, Parmesan and salt. Stir the oil into 280 ml / 9 fl. oz / 1 cup of warm water, then stir it into the dry ingredients.

2. Knead the mixture on a lightly oiled surface for 10 minutes or until smooth and elastic. Leave the dough to rest, covered with oiled cling film, for 1–2 hours or until doubled in size.

3. Knead two-thirds of the Gruyère into the dough, then divide it into 2 pieces. Shape each piece into a leaf, then make deep slashes where the veins would be. Transfer the fougasse to a greased baking tray, then cover with oiled cling film and leave to prove for 1 hour or until doubled in size.

4. Preheat the oven to 220°C (200°C fan) / 425F / gas 7.

5. Sprinkle the rest of the cheese over the fougasse. Transfer the tray to the top shelf of the oven.

6. Bake for 25 minutes or until the bread loaves sounds hollow when you tap them underneath. Transfer to a wire rack and brush with olive oil, then leave to cool completely before serving.

TOP TIP
Try dipping the warm fougasse into green olive tapenade.

azelnut and
ig Rolls

ES **12 ROLLS**

PARATION TIME **2 HOURS 30 MINUTES**

KING TIME **15 MINUTES**

REDIENTS

g / 14 oz / 2 ⅔ cups strong white bread flour,
lus extra for dusting
p easy-blend dried yeast
sp caster (superfine) sugar
fine sea salt
/ 2 ½ oz / ⅓ cup dried figs, chopped
1 ¾ oz / ½ cup hazelnuts (cobnuts), chopped
sp olive oil

METHOD

1. Mix together the flour, yeast, sugar, salt, figs and hazelnuts. Stir the oil into 280 ml / 9 fl. oz / 1 cup of warm water, then stir it into the dry ingredients.

2. Knead the mixture on a lightly oiled surface for 10 minutes or until smooth and elastic. Leave the dough to rest, covered with oiled cling film, for 1–2 hours or until doubled in size.

3. Shape the dough into 12 rolls and transfer to a greased baking tray, then cover with oiled cling film and leave to prove for 1 hour or until doubled in size.

4. Preheat the oven to 220°C (200°C fan) / 425F / gas 7.

5. Dust the rolls with a little flour and slash the top of each one with a sharp knife. Transfer the tray to the top shelf of the oven, then close the door.

6. Bake for 15 minutes or until the rolls sound hollow when you tap them underneath. Transfer to a wire rack and leave to cool completely before serving.

TOP TIP
These rolls taste great filled with mature Cheddar.

Cakes and Muffins

Mixed Fruit Scones

MAKES 12

PREPARATION TIME 25 MINUTES

COOKING TIME 15–20 MINUTES

INGREDIENTS

225 g / 8 oz / 1 ½ cups self-raising flour
55 g / 2 oz / ¼ cup butter
75 g / 2 ½ oz / ½ cup mixed dried fruit
150 ml / 5 fl. oz / ⅔ cup whole milk

METHOD

1. Preheat the oven to 220°C (200°C fan) / 425F / gas 7 and oil a large baking tray.

2. Sieve the flour into a bowl and rub in the butter until the mixture resembles fine breadcrumbs. Add the mixed fruit and stir in enough milk to bring the mixture together into a soft dough.

3. Flatten the dough with your hands on a floured work surface into a 2.5 cm (1 in) thick rectangle. Transfer it to the baking tray and score into 12 squares.

4. Bake in the oven for 15–20 minutes or until golden brown and cooked through. Transfer the scones to a wire rack to cool a little, then break into squares and serve with jam.

TOP TIP
Try replacing the dried fruit with chocolate chips.

hocolate nd Hazelnut almiers

ES 12

PARATION TIME **15 MINUTES**

KING TIME **20 MINUTES**

REDIENTS

3 / 9 oz / 1 cup all-butter puff pastry
3 / 3 ½ oz / ½ cup chocolate and hazelnut
obnut) spread

METHOD

1. Preheat the oven to 220°C (200°C fan) / 430F / gas 7 and line a baking tray with greaseproof paper.

2. Roll out the pastry on a floured surface into a large rectangle. Spread the top of the pastry with chocolate and hazelnut spread, then roll it up into a tight sausage. Cut the roll across into 12 slices, then transfer them to the prepared baking tray.

3. Bake in the oven for 20 minutes or until golden brown and cooked through, then transfer the pastries to a wire rack to cool a little and serve warm.

TOP TIP

Try replacing the chocolate spread with fruit jam (jelly) or compote.

Oat and Cranberry Muffins

MAKES 12

PREPARATION TIME 25 MINUTES

COOKING TIME 20–25 MINUTES

INGREDIENTS

1 large egg
120 ml / 4 fl. oz / ½ cup sunflower oil
120 ml / 4 fl. oz / ½ cup milk
375 g / 12 ½ oz / 2 ½ cups wholemeal self-raising
    flour, sifted
1 tsp baking powder
1 tsp mixed spice
200 g / 7 oz / ¾ cup caster (superfine) sugar
75 g / 2 ½ oz / ½ cup dried cranberries
75 g / 2 ½ oz / ½ cup porridge oats

METHOD

1. Preheat the oven to 180°C (160°C fan) / 350F / gas 4 and line 12 mini pudding basins with squares of greaseproof paper.

2. Beat the egg in a jug with the oil and milk until well mixed. Mix the flour, baking powder, spice, sugar, cranberries and oats in a bowl, then pour in the egg mixture and stir just enough to combine.

3. Divide the mixture between the cases, then bake in the oven for 20–25 minutes. Test with a wooden toothpick, if it comes out clean, the cakes are done. Leave to cool before serving.

TOP TIP
Try replacing the cranberries with raisins for a classic combination.

herry and azelnut uffins

ES 12

PARATION TIME 20 MINUTES

KING TIME 20–25 MINUTES

REDIENTS

ge egg

ange, zest finely grated

ml / 4 ½ fl. oz / ½ cup sunflower oil

ml / 4 ½ fl. oz / ½ cup milk

g / 13 oz / 2 ½ cups self-raising flour, sifted

baking powder

g / 7 oz / ¾ cup caster (superfine) sugar

/ 2 ½ oz / ⅓ cup glacé cherries, quartered

/ 1 ¾ oz / ½ cup hazelnuts (cobnuts), chopped

METHOD

1. Preheat the oven to 180°C (160°C fan) / 350F / gas 4 and grease a 12-square-hole silicone muffin mould.

2. Beat the egg in a jug with the orange zest, oil and milk until well mixed.

3. Mix the flour, baking powder and sugar in a bowl, then pour in the egg mixture, chopped cherries and hazelnuts and stir just enough to combine.

4. Spoon the mixture into the mould, then bake in the oven for 20–25 minutes. Test with a wooden toothpick, if it comes out clean, the cakes are done. Transfer the cakes to a wire rack and leave to cool completely.

TOP TIP

Drizzle the muffins with a little glacé icing for a pretty presentation.

Apple Mini Muffins

MAKES **12**

PREPARATION TIME **25 MINUTES**

COOKING TIME **15–20 MINUTES**

INGREDIENTS

1 large egg
120 ml / 4 fl. oz / ½ cup sunflower oil
120 ml / 4 fl. oz / ½ cup milk
375 g / 12 ½ oz / 2 ½ cups self-raising flour, sifted
1 tsp baking powder
1 tsp ground ginger
200 g / 7 oz / ¾ cup caster (superfine) sugar
150 g / 5 oz / 1 cup eating apple, thinly sliced

METHOD

1. Preheat the oven to 180°C (160°C fan) / 350F / gas 4 and line a 12-hole cupcake tin with paper cases.

2. Beat the egg in a jug with the oil and milk until well mixed. Mix the flour, baking powder, ginger and sugar in a bowl, then pour in the egg mixture and stir just enou to combine. Reserve 12 apple slices and f the rest into the mixture.

3. Divide the mixture between the paper cas and top with the reserved apple slices, th bake in the oven for 15–20 minutes.

4. Test with a wooden toothpick, if it comes c clean, the cakes are done. Transfer the cak to a wire rack and leave to cool completel

TOP TIP
Try serving the muffins with cinnamon spiced whipped cream.

Wholemeal Blueberry Muffins

KES 12

PARATION TIME 25 MINUTES

OKING TIME 20–25 MINUTES

GREDIENTS

- rge egg
- ml / 4 fl. oz / ½ cup sunflower oil
- ml / 4 fl. oz / ½ cup whole milk
- g / 12 ½ oz / 2 ½ cups wholemeal self-raising lour, sifted
- p baking powder
- p mixed spice
- g / 7 oz / ¾ cup caster (superfine) sugar
- g / 3 ½ oz / ⅔ cup blueberries
- sp sugar nibs

METHOD

1. Preheat the oven to 180°C (160°C fan) / 350F / gas 4 and line 12 mini pudding basins with squares of greaseproof paper.

2. Beat the egg in a jug with the oil and milk until well mixed. Mix the flour, baking powder, spice, sugar and blueberries in a bowl, then pour in the egg mixture and stir just enough to combine.

3. Divide the mixture between the paper cases and sprinkle with sugar nibs, then bake in the oven for 20–25 minutes. Test with a wooden toothpick, if it comes out clean, the cakes are done. Leave to cool before serving.

TOP TIP

Try adding the finely grated zest of an orange to the cake mixture for added zing.

Raisin Scones with Cream and Jam

MAKES 12

PREPARATION TIME 25 MINUTES

COOKING TIME 25 MINUTES

INGREDIENTS

225 g / 8 oz / 1 ½ cups self-raising flour
55 g / 2 oz / ¼ cup butter, plus extra for spreading
75 g / 2 ½ oz / ⅓ cup raisins
150 ml / 5 fl. oz / ⅔ cup whole milk
1 egg, beaten
200 g / 7 oz / ¾ cup double (heavy) cream
200 g / 7 oz / ¾ cup strawberry jam (jelly)

METHOD

1. Preheat the oven to 220°C (200°C fan) / 425F / gas 7 and oil a large baking tray.

2. Sieve the flour into a bowl and rub in the butter until the mixture resembles fine breadcrumbs. Stir in the raisins with enough milk to bring the mixture together into a soft dough.

3. Flatten the dough with your hands on a floured work surface until 2.5 cm (1 in) thick. Use a pastry cutter to cut out 12 circles and transfer them to the prepared baking tray.

4. Brush the scones with beaten egg, then bake for 15 minutes or until golden brown and cooked through. Transfer the scones to a wire rack to cool completely.

5. Whip the cream until it just holds its shape. When the scones have cooled, spread them with butter and jam, then spoon a little whipped cream on top.

TOP TIP
For a healthier alternative, replace the cream with thick Greek yogurt.

hocolate Chip upcakes with lueberries

ES 6

PARATION TIME **35 MINUTES**

KING TIME **15–20 MINUTES**

REDIENTS

/ 4 oz / ⅔ cup self-raising flour, sifted
baking powder
/ 4 oz / ½ cup caster (superfine) sugar
/ 4 oz / ½ cup butter, softened
ge eggs
vanilla extract
/ 2 ½ oz / ½ cup chocolate chips

ecorate
/ 3 ½ oz / 1 cup icing (confectioners') sugar
/ 3 ½ oz / ⅔ cup blueberries

METHOD

1. Preheat the oven to 190°C (170°C fan) / 375F / gas 5 and line a 6-hole muffin tin with paper cases.

2. Combine the flour, baking powder, sugar, butter, eggs and vanilla extract in a bowl and whisk together for 2 minutes or until smooth. Stir in the chocolate chips.

3. Divide the mixture between the cases, then transfer the tin to the oven and bake for 20–25 minutes. Test with a wooden toothpick, if it comes out clean, the cakes are done. Transfer the cakes to a wire rack and leave to cool completely.

4. Add cold water a few drops at a time to the icing sugar until you get a pourable icing, then spoon it over the cakes and sprinkle with blueberries.

TOP TIP
Replace the glacé icing with melted white chocolate.

Madeleines

MAKES **12**

PREPARATION TIME **1 HOUR 15 MINUTES**

COOKING TIME **10–15 MINUTES**

INGREDIENTS

110 g / 4 oz / ½ cup butter
55 g / 2 oz / ⅓ cup plain (all-purpose) flour
55 g / 2 oz / ½ cup ground almonds
110 g / 4 oz / 1 cup icing (confectioners') sugar
3 large egg whites

METHOD

1. Heat the butter until it foams and starts to smell nutty, then leave to cool.

2. Combine the flour, ground almonds and icing sugar in a bowl and whisk in the egg whites. Pour the cooled butter through a sieve into the bowl and whisk into the mixture. Leave the cake mixture to rest in the fridge for 1 hour.

3. Preheat the oven to 170°C (150°C fan) / 325F / gas 3 and oil and flour a 12-hole madeleine mould.

4. Spoon the mixture into the moulds, then transfer the tin to the oven and bake for 10–15 minutes.

5. Test with a wooden toothpick, if it comes out clean, the cakes are done. Transfer to a wire rack to cool.

TOP TIP

Try serving the madeleines with hot butterscotch sauce for dipping.

lmond Choux Buns

KES 8

EPARATION TIME 45 MINUTES

KING TIME 20 MINUTES

GREDIENTS

- / 2 oz / ¼ cup butter, cubed
- / 2 ½ oz / ½ cup strong white bread
  flour, sieved
- rge eggs, beaten
- / 2 ½ oz / ⅔ cup flaked (slivered) almonds
  ml / 8 fl. oz / 1 cup double (heavy) cream
- sp amaretto liqueur
- g (confectioners') sugar to dust

METHOD

1. Preheat the oven to 200°C (180°C fan) / 400F / gas 6. Oil and line a large baking tray with greaseproof paper, then spray it with water.

2. Bring the butter and 150 ml / 5 fl. oz / ⅔ cup cold water to the boil, then beat in the flour off the heat. Continue to beat until you have a smooth ball of pastry that leaves the sides of the saucepan clean. Stir in the beaten egg a little at a time to make a glossy paste.

3. Spoon the pastry into a piping bag fitted with a large star nozzle and pipe 8 buns onto the tray. Sprinkle with almonds and bake for 20 minutes, increasing the heat to 220°C (200°C fan) / 425F / gas 7 halfway through.

4. Transfer the choux buns to a wire rack, cut in half horizontally and leave to cool completely.

5. Whip the cream with the amaretto until thick, then spoon into a piping bag fitted with a large star nozzle. Sandwich the choux buns back together with the cream, then dust liberally with icing sugar.

TOP TIP
Try replacing the almonds with hazelnuts (cobnuts).

Almond Pain au Chocolat

MAKES 6

PREPARATION TIME **15 MINUTES**

COOKING TIME **10 MINUTES**

INGREDIENTS

55 g / 2 oz / ½ cup ground almonds
55 g / 2 oz / ¼ cup caster (superfine) sugar
55 g / 2 oz / ¼ cup butter, softened
1 large egg
½ tsp almond essence
6 pain au chocolat
3 tbsp flaked (slivered) almonds
icing (confectioners') sugar for dusting

METHOD

1. Preheat the oven to 200°C (180°C fan) / 400F / gas 6.

2. Combine the ground almonds, sugar, butter, egg and almond essence in a bowl and whisk for 2 minutes or until smooth.

3. Cut open each pain au chocolat and spread a spoonful of the almond mixture inside. Transfer to a baking tray and spoon the rest of the mixture over the top.

4. Sprinkle with flaked almonds and bake for 10 minutes or until the tops are golden brown. Dust with icing sugar before serving.

TOP TIP
You can use the almond mixture to fill croissants too.

…hocolate and …azelnut Mini …upcakes

…ES 24

…PARATION TIME **15 MINUTES**

…KING TIME **12–15 MINUTES**

…REDIENTS

…g / 4 oz / ⅔ cup self-raising flour, sifted

…g / 4 oz / ½ cup caster (superfine) sugar

…g / 4 oz / ½ cup butter, softened

…ge eggs

…sp unsweetened cocoa powder

…/ 1 ¾ oz / ½ cup hazelnuts (cobnuts), chopped

METHOD

1. Preheat the oven to 190°C (170°C fan) / 375F / gas 5 and line a 24-hole mini cupcake tin with paper cases.

2. Combine the flour, sugar, butter, eggs, cocoa powder and three quarters of the hazelnuts in a bowl and whisk together for 2 minutes or until smooth.

3. Divide the mixture between the cases, then transfer the tin to the oven and bake for 12–15 minutes. Test with a wooden toothpick, if it comes out clean, the cakes are done.

4. Transfer the cakes to a wire rack, sprinkle over the rest of the hazelnuts and leave to cool completely.

TOP TIP

Spread the muffins with chocolate and hazelnut spread for a quick icing.

Chocolate Chip and Oat Bran Muffins

MAKES 12

PREPARATION TIME 15 MINUTES

COOKING TIME 20–25 MINUTES

INGREDIENTS

1 large egg
120 ml / 4 fl. oz / ½ cup sunflower oil
120 ml / 4 fl. oz / ½ cup milk
375 g / 12 ½ oz / 2 ½ cups wholemeal self-raising
    flour, sifted
1 tsp baking powder
200 g / 7 oz / ¾ cup caster (superfine) sugar
75 g / 2 ½ oz / ½ cup chocolate chips
4 tbsp oat bran

METHOD

1. Preheat the oven to 180°C (160°C fan) / 350F / gas 4 and line a 12-hole muffin tin with muffin wrappers.

2. Beat the egg in a jug with the oil and milk until well mixed. Mix the flour, baking powder, sugar, chocolate chips and half of the oat bran in a bowl, then pour in the egg mixture and stir just enough to combine.

3. Divide the mixture between the wrappers and sprinkle the tops with the rest of the oat bran, then bake in the oven for 20–25 minutes. Test with a wooden toothpick, if it comes out clean, the cakes are done. Leave to cool before serving.

TOP TIP
Add 3 tbsp of chopped stem ginger for a spicy warmth.

hocolate nd Sesame luffins

ES 12

PARATION TIME **15 MINUTES**

KING TIME **15–25 MINUTES**

REDIENTS

ge egg

nl / 3 ½ fl. oz / ½ cup sunflower oil

p sesame oil

nl / 4 ½ fl. oz / ½ cup milk

/ 12 ½ oz / 2 ⅓ cups self-raising flour, sifted

1 ¾ oz / ½ cup unsweetened cocoa

wder, sifted

baking powder

/ 7 oz / ¾ cup caster (superfine) sugar

p sesame seeds

METHOD

1. Preheat the oven to 180°C (160°C fan) / 350F / gas 4 and grease 12 mini pudding basins.

2. Beat the egg in a jug with the oils and milk until well mixed.

3. Mix the flour, cocoa, baking powder and sugar in a bowl, then pour in the egg mixture and stir just enough to combine.

4. Divide the mixture between the cases and sprinkle with sesame seeds, then bake in the oven for 20–25 minutes. Test with a wooden toothpick, if it comes out clean, the cakes are done. Serve warm or leave to cool on a wire rack.

TOP TIP
Try adding 3 tbsp of chopped pistachio nuts to the mixture.

Ginger Cupcakes with Ginger Buttercream

MAKES 12

PREPARATION TIME 45 MINUTES

COOKING TIME 15–20 MINUTES

INGREDIENTS

110 g / 4 oz / ²/₃ cup self-raising flour, sifted
110 g / 4 oz / ½ cup caster (superfine) sugar
110 g / 4 oz / ½ cup butter, softened
2 tsp ground ginger
2 large eggs
3 pieces of stem ginger, finely chopped
2 tbsp stem ginger syrup

To decorate
100 g / 3 ½ oz / ½ cup butter, softened
200 g / 7 oz / 2 cups icing (confectioners') sugar
1 tbsp stem ginger syrup
1 tsp ground ginger
2 ginger-nut biscuits, crumbled

METHOD

1. Preheat the oven to 190°C (170°C fan) / 375F / gas 5 and line a 12-hole cupcake tin with paper cases.

2. Combine the flour, sugar, butter, ground ginger, eggs and stem ginger in a bowl and whisk together for 2 minutes or until smooth.

3. Divide the mixture between the cases, then transfer the tin to the oven and bake for 15–20 minutes. Test with a wooden toothpick, if it comes out clean, the cakes are done.

4. Transfer the cakes to a wire rack, brush with ginger syrup and leave to cool completely.

5. Beat the butter until smooth, then gradually whisk in the icing sugar, ginger syrup and ground ginger. Spoon the buttercream into a piping bag, fitted with a large plain nozzle, and pipe it onto the cakes. Crumble over the ginger-nut biscuits.

TOP TIP
Add the finely grated zest of a lime to the cake mixture and icing for added zing.

lain
uttercream
upcakes

ES 12

PARATION TIME **45 MINUTES**

KING TIME **15–20 MINUTES**

REDIENTS

g / 4 oz / ⅔ cup self-raising flour, sifted

g / 4 oz / ½ cup caster (superfine) sugar

g / 4 oz / ½ cup butter, softened

ge eggs

vanilla extract

ecorate

g / 3 ½ oz / ½ cup butter, softened

g / 7 oz / 2 cups icing (confectioners') sugar

METHOD

1. Preheat the oven to 190°C (170°C fan) / 375F / gas 5 and line a 12-hole cupcake tin with paper cases.

2. Combine the flour, sugar, butter, eggs and vanilla extract in a bowl and whisk together for 2 minutes or until smooth.

3. Divide the mixture between the cases, then transfer the tin to the oven and bake for 15–20 minutes. Test with a wooden toothpick, if it comes out clean, the cakes are done. Transfer the cakes to a wire rack and leave to cool completely.

4. Beat the butter until smooth, then gradually whisk in the icing sugar. If the icing is too stiff, add a teaspoon or two of warm water and beat well. Use a palette knife to spread the buttercream onto the cakes.

TOP TIP

Serve with sweets and dried fruit so that guests can decorate their own cupcake.

Strawberry Eclairs

MAKES 12

PREPARATION TIME 45 MINUTES

COOKING TIME 20 MINUTES

INGREDIENTS

55 g / 2 oz / ¼ cup butter, cubed
70 g / 2 ½ oz / ½ cup strong white bread flour, sieved
2 large eggs, beaten

For the filling

600 ml / 1 pint / 2 ½ cups double (heavy) cream
2 tbsp icing (confectioners') sugar, plus extra for dusting
200 g / 7 oz / 1 ⅓ cups strawberries, hulled

METHOD

1. Preheat the oven to 200°C (180°C fan) / 400F / gas 6. Oil and line a large baking tray with greaseproof paper, then spray with a little water.

2. Put the butter in a saucepan with 150 ml 5 fl. oz / ⅔ cup cold water and heat until butter melts and the water starts to boil Turn off the heat and beat in the flour.

3. Continue to beat the mixture until it form smooth ball of pastry. Stir in the beaten e a little at a time until you have a glossy p

4. Spoon the pastry into a piping bag with a large plain nozzle and pipe 12 cm (5 in) li onto the prepared baking tray.

5. Bake for 10 minutes, then increase the heat to 220°C (200°C fan) / 425F / gas 7 a bake for another 10 minutes. Transfer to wire rack and slice down one side of eac one so the steam can escape. Leave to cool completely.

6. Whip the cream with the icing sugar unti thick. Spoon the cream into a piping bag fitted with a large star nozzle and fill the eclairs. Stud each one with strawberries Dust the tops with icing sugar and serve.

TOP TIP

Use raspberries and add a splash of rose water to the cream.

rofiteroles

METHOD

1. Preheat the oven to 200°C (180°C fan) / 400F / gas 6. Line a baking tray with greaseproof paper and spray with a little bit of water.

2. Melt the butter with 150 ml / 5 fl. oz / ⅔ cup water and bring to the boil. Turn off the heat. Immediately beat in the flour with a wooden spoon until it forms a smooth ball of pastry. Incorporate the egg a little at a time to make a glossy paste.

3. Spoon the pastry into a piping bag fitted with a large plain nozzle and pipe 2.5 cm (1 in) buns onto the baking tray.

4. Bake for 20 minutes, increasing the temperature to 220°C (200°C fan) / 425F / gas 7 halfway through. Transfer to a wire rack and make a hole in the underneath of each one so the steam can escape. Leave to cool completely.

5. Whip the cream until thick, then spoon it into a piping bag and fill the choux buns through the steam hole.

6. Stir a few drops of water into the icing sugar until you get a pourable icing then drizzle it over the profiteroles. Squeeze over the chocolate sauce, then sprinkle with white chocolate sprinkles.

ES 24

PARATION TIME 45 MINUTES

KING TIME 20 MINUTES

REDIENTS

/ 2 oz / ¼ cup butter, cubed

/ 2 ½ oz / ½ cup strong white bread flour, ieved

ge eggs, beaten

ml / 8 fl. oz / 1 cup double (heavy) cream

g / 3 ½ oz / 1 cup icing (confectioners') sugar

ml / 3 ½ fl. oz / ½ cup chocolate sauce

sp white chocolate sprinkles

TOP TIP

Don't make the choux buns too large, as they may not cook all the way through.

Lemon Meringue Pies

MAKES 6

PREPARATION TIME 1 HOUR

COOKING TIME 30 MINUTES

INGREDIENTS

100 g / 3 ½ oz / ½ cup butter, cubed
200 g / 7 oz / 1 ⅓ cups plain (all-purpose) flour
225 g / 8 oz / 1 cup lemon curd
4 large egg whites
110 g / 4 oz / ½ cup caster (superfine) sugar

METHOD

1. Preheat the oven to 200°C (180°C fan) / 400F / gas 6.

2. Rub the butter into the flour and add just enough cold water to bind. Chill for 30 minutes, then roll out on a floured surface and cut out 6 circles with a large round cookie cutter. Use the pastry circle to line a 6-hole deep muffin tin and prick the bases with a fork.

3. Line the pastry with cling film and fill with baking beans or rice, then bake for 10 minutes. Remove the cling film and beans and cook for another 8 minutes to crisp. Fill the pastry cases with lemon cu

4. Whisk the egg whites until stiff, then gradually add the sugar and whisk until the mixture is thick and shiny. Spoon the meringue into a piping bag fitted with a large star nozzle and pipe a swirl on top of each pie. Return the tin to the oven to bake for 10 minutes or until golden brown. Serve hot or cold.

TOP TIP

These pies are also delicious filled with passion fruit curd.

emon and hocolate ray Bake

VES 9

PARATION TIME **1 HOUR**

KING TIME **30 MINUTES**

REDIENTS

cornflour (cornstarch)
nons, zest and juice
ge eggs, beaten
g / 8 oz / 1 cup butter
g / 6 oz / ¾ cup caster (superfine) sugar

he pastry

g / 3 ½ oz / ½ cup butter, cubed
g / 7 oz / 1 ⅓ cups plain (all-purpose) flour
/ 2 oz / ½ cup caster (superfine) sugar
g, beaten

ecorate

g / 7 oz / 1 ¼ cups dark chocolate (minimum
0% cocoa solids), chopped
/ 1 ¾ oz / ½ cup butter

METHOD

1. Preheat the oven to 200°C (180°C fan) / 390F / gas 6.

2. For the pastry, rub the butter into the flour and sugar, then add the egg with just enough cold water to bind. Wrap the dough in cling film and chill for 30 minutes, then roll out on a floured surface.

3. Use the pastry to line the bottom of a 23 cm (9 in) square cake tin and trim the edges. Prick the pastry with a fork, line with cling film and fill with baking beans or rice. Bake for 10 minutes, then remove the cling film and baking beans and cook for another 8 minutes.

4. Meanwhile, dissolve the cornflour in the lemon juice and put it in a saucepan with the rest of the ingredients. Stir over a medium heat; after 6 or 7 minutes the mixture should thicken. Continue until it starts to bubble then spoon it onto the pastry base and level with a palette knife. Leave to cool completely.

5. Put the chocolate and butter in a bowl set over a pan of simmering water and stir together until melted.

6. Pour the mixture over the lemon layer and leave to cool and set before cutting into 9 squares.

TOP TIP

Use white chocolate instead and sprinkle with chopped almonds before it sets.

Chocolate and Hazelnut Brownies

MAKES 16

PREPARATION TIME 5 MINUTES

COOKING TIME 35 MINUTES

INGREDIENTS

110 g / 4 oz / ⅔ cup dark chocolate (minimum
    70% cocoa solids), chopped
85 g / 3 oz / ¾ cup unsweetened cocoa powder,
    sifted
225 g / 8 oz / 1 cup butter
450 g / 1 lb / 2 ½ cups light brown sugar
4 large eggs
110 g / 4 oz / 1 cup self-raising flour
75 g / 2 ½ oz / ½ cup toasted hazelnuts
    (cobnuts), chopped

METHOD

1. Preheat the oven to 160°C (140°C fan)
   / 325F / gas 3 and oil and line a 20 cm
   x 20 cm (8 in x 8 in) square cake tin.

2. Melt the chocolate, cocoa and butter in
   a saucepan, then leave to cool a little.

3. Whisk the sugar and eggs together with
   an electric whisk for 3 minutes or until
   very light and creamy.

4. Pour in the chocolate mixture and sieve
   over the flour. Reserve 1 tbsp of the nuts
   to decorate and fold the rest into the
   brownie batter.

5. Scrape into the tin and bake for 35 minutes
   or until the outside is set, but the centre
   still quite soft.

6. Leave the brownie to cool completely before
   cutting into 12 squares and sprinkling with
   the reserved hazelnuts.

TOP TIP
Stir the grated zest of an orange through the mixture for chocolate orange brownies.

each Cake with Lemon hyme Sugar

VES 8

PARATION TIME **15 MINUTES**

KING TIME **55 MINUTES**

REDIENTS

g / 8 oz / 1 ½ cups self-raising flour
g / 3 ½ oz / ½ cup butter, cubed
g / 3 ½ oz / ½ cup caster (superfine) sugar
ge egg
l / 2 ½ fl. oz / ⅓ cup whole milk
aches, halved and stoned

the lemon thyme sugar

sp lemon thyme leaves
/ 2 oz / ¼ cup caster (superfine) sugar

METHOD

1. Preheat the oven to 180°C (160°C fan) / 350F / gas 4 and butter a large round baking dish.

2. First make the lemon thyme sugar. Bruise the thyme leaves with a mortar and pestle, then add half the sugar and pound again. Stir in the rest of the sugar and set aside.

3. Sieve the flour into a mixing bowl and rub in the butter until it resembles fine breadcrumbs, then stir in the sugar.

4. Lightly beat the egg with the milk and stir it into the dry ingredients until just combined.

5. Scrape the mixture into the baking dish and level the surface, then press in the peach halves, cut side up.

6. Bake the cake for 55 minutes or until a skewer inserted comes out clean.

7. Transfer the cake to a wire rack and sprinkle with the lemon thyme sugar, then leave to cool completely.

TOP TIP
Use edible lavender flowers for a more aromatic but delicious cake.

Wholemeal Walnut Loaf Cake

SERVES 8

PREPARATION TIME 15 MINUTES

COOKING TIME 35–40 MINUTES

INGREDIENTS

100 g / 3 ½ oz / ⅔ cup stoneground wholemeal
    flour
50 g / 1 ¾ oz / ½ cup ground walnuts
2 tsp baking powder
150 g / 5 ½ oz / ⅔ cup caster (superfine) sugar
150 g / 5 ½ oz / ⅔ cup butter
3 large eggs
1 tsp ground cinnamon
1 tsp ground ginger
½ tsp freshly grated nutmeg
8 walnut halves
pouring cream to serve

METHOD

1. Preheat the oven to 180°C (160°C fan) / 3
   / gas 4 and grease and line a small loaf t

2. Put all of the ingredients, except for the
   walnut halves, in a large mixing bowl an
   whisk them together with an electric wh
   for 4 minutes or until pale and well whipp

3. Scrape the mixture into the tin and level
   the top with a spatula, then lay the walnu
   halves on top in a line down the middle.

4. Bake for 35–40 minutes. The cake is rea
   when a toothpick inserted in the centre
   comes out clean. Transfer the cake to a
   wire rack to cool completely before slicir
   and serving with pouring cream.

TOP TIP

Try adding a handful of chopped, dried pear to the cake mixture before baking.

Orange Syrup Loaf Cake

ERVES 8

EPARATION TIME 30 MINUTES

OKING TIME 55 MINUTES

GREDIENTS

g / 8 oz / 1 ½ cups self-raising flour
g / 3 ½ oz / ½ cup butter, cubed
g / 3 oz / ⅓ cup caster (superfine) sugar
ranges, juiced and zest finely grated
rge egg

the topping
ranges, juiced
g / 3 ½ oz / ½ cup caster (superfine) sugar
andied orange slices

1. P
/ 3
gre

2. Siev
rub ir
bread
orange
the orar
ingredier

Lemon
Por

3. Scrape th   oaf tin and
bake for 55   es or until a skewer
inserted in the centre comes out clean.

4. While the cake is cooking, put the sugar
and orange juice into a small saucepan
and stir over a low heat until the sugar
dissolves. Increase the heat and simmer
without stirring for 4 minutes or until
syrupy. Stir in the candied orange slices.

5. When the cake comes out of the oven,
arrange the orange slices on top and
spoon over the hot syrup. Leave to soak
until the cake has cooled completely
before unmoulding.

TOP TIP

This cake will keep well
in an air-tight tin for up
to 1 week.

...and ...ppy Seed Cake

SERVES 8

PREPARATION TIME 15 MINUTES

COOKING TIME 55 MINUTES

INGREDIENTS

225 g / 8 oz / 1 ½ cups self-raising flour
100 g / 3 ½ oz / ½ cup butter, cubed
100 g / 3 ½ oz / ½ cup caster (superfine) sugar
3 tbsp poppy seeds
1 large egg
75 ml / 2 ½ fl. oz / ⅓ cup whole milk
1 lemon, juiced and zest finely grated

METHOD

1. Preheat the oven to 180°C (160°C fan) / 355F / gas 4 and line a 18 cm (7 in) round cake tin with greaseproof paper.

2. Sieve the flour into a mixing bowl and rub in the butter until it resembles fine breadcrumbs, then stir in the sugar and poppy seeds.

3. Lightly beat the egg with the milk, lemon juice and lemon zest and stir it into the dry ingredients until just combined.

4. Scrape the mixture into the tin and bake for 55 minutes or until a skewer inserted into the centre comes out clean. Transfer the cake to a wire rack and leave to cool completely.

TOP TIP

Make an easy icing by stirring a few drops of lemon juice into sieved icing sugar.

offee and ut-topped inger Cake

ES 8

ARATION TIME **30 MINUTES**

KING TIME **35–40 MINUTES**

REDIENTS

/ 9 oz / 1 ⅔ cups self-raising flour
bicarbonate of (baking) soda
ground ginger
/ 5 ½ oz / ½ cup golden syrup
1 ¾ oz / ¼ cup treacle
/ 4 ½ oz / ½ cup butter
/ 4 ½ oz / ¾ cup dark brown sugar
ge eggs, beaten
ml / 9 fl. oz / 1 cup milk

he topping
3 oz / ½ cup butter
3 oz / ¼ cup golden syrup
3 oz / ½ cup dark brown sugar
1 ¾ oz / ½ cup walnuts, chopped
1 ¾ oz / ½ cup hazelnuts (cobnuts), chopped

METHOD

1. Preheat the oven to 180°C (160°C fan) / 355F / gas 4 and grease and line a loaf tin.

2. Sieve the flour, bicarbonate of soda and ginger into a bowl. Put the golden syrup, treacle, butter and brown sugar in a small saucepan and boil gently for 2 minutes, stirring to dissolve the sugar. Add the butter and sugar mixture to the flour with the eggs and milk and fold it all together until smooth.

3. Scrape the mixture into the prepared tin and bake for 35–40 minutes. The cake is ready when a toothpick inserted in the centre comes out clean. Transfer the cake to a wire rack to cool completely.

4. To make the topping, put the butter, syrup and sugar in a saucepan and stir over a low heat to dissolve the sugar. Increase the heat and simmer without stirring for 3 minutes or until thick. Stir in the nuts then leave to cool a little before spooning it over the cake.

TOP TIP

Try folding two chopped pears through the cake mixture before baking.

Blueberry Bundt Cakes

MAKES *8*

PREPARATION TIME **15 MINUTES**

COOKING TIME **25 MINUTES**

INGREDIENTS

225 g / 8 oz / 1 cup butter, softened
225 g / 8 oz / 1 cup caster (superfine) sugar
4 large eggs, beaten
150 g / 5 ½ oz / 1 cup self-raising flour
75 g / 2 ½ oz / ½ cup blueberries

METHOD

1. Preheat the oven to 180°C (160°C fan) / 350F / gas 4 and butter 8 mini bundt tin or other decorative moulds.

2. Cream the butter and sugar together un well whipped, then whisk in the eggs in batches, beating well after each additio

3. Fold in the flour and blueberries, then divide the mixture between the tins. Bake the cakes for 25 minutes or until a skewer inserted in the centre comes o clean. Turn the cakes out onto a wire rac and leave to cool completely.

TOP TIP
Serve the cakes with warm orange custard.

iant Rum aba

ES 6

ARATION TIME **2 HOURS**

ING TIME **20–30 MINUTES**

REDIENTS

/ 5 oz / 1 cup plain (all-purpose) flour
easy-blend dried yeast
caster (superfine) sugar
salt
ge eggs, lightly beaten
2 ½ oz / ⅓ cup butter, softened

he soaking syrup

/ 1 lb / 2 cups caster (superfine) sugar
l / 9 fl. oz / 1 cup rum

corate

l / 9 fl. oz / 1 cup double (heavy) cream
paya, peeled, deseeded and thinly sliced
awberries, sliced
pberries, halved

METHOD

1. Oil a 23 cm (9 in) ring mould. Combine the flour, yeast, sugar and salt in a bowl and gradually whisk in half of the beaten egg with an electric whisk. Continuing to whisk, incorporate half of the butter, followed by the rest of the egg. Beat the remaining butter in with a wooden spoon, then spoon the mixture into the mould.

2. Leave the baba to prove in a warm, draught-free place for 1 hour or until it has double in size. Preheat the oven to 200°C (180°C fan) / 400F / gas 6.

3. Bake the baba for 20–30 minutes or until golden brown and cooked through, then turn it out onto a wire rack.

4. Put the sugar in a saucepan with 675 ml / 1 pint 4 fl. oz / 2 ¾ cups water and stir over a medium heat to dissolve the sugar. Boil the sugar water for 5 minutes or until it starts to turn syrupy, then stir in the rum.

5. Transfer the baba to a mixing bowl, pour over the syrup and leave to soak until cold, turning occasionally.

6. Whip the cream until it holds its shape. Transfer the baba to a serving plate and top with the fruit and quenelles of cream.

TOP TIP
Try using coconut rum and top the baba with tropical fruit.

Steamed Fruit Cake

SERVES 8

PREPARATION TIME 35 MINUTES

PLUS OVERNIGHT SOAKING

COOKING TIME 3 HOURS

INGREDIENTS

350 g / 12 oz / 1 ¾ cups mixed dried fruit
55 ml / 2 fl. oz / ¼ cup brandy
110 g / 4 oz / ½ cup butter, softened
2 tbsp treacle
110 g / 4 oz / ½ cup dark brown sugar
2 large eggs, beaten
55 g / 2 oz / ⅓ cup self-raising flour
2 tsp mixed spice
1 tbsp ground almonds
pouring cream to serve

METHOD

1. Mix the dried fruit with the brandy and l[
   to macerate overnight.

2. Cream the butter, treacle and sugar
   together until well whipped, then gradu
   whisk in the eggs, beating well after eac
   addition. Sift over the flour and spice an
   fold in with the ground almonds and
   dried fruit.

3. Scrape the mixture into a large buttere[
   pudding basin. Add a pleated sheet of
   buttered foil to the top and tie securely
   with string to make a handle.

4. Steam the cake for 3 hours, making sur[
   check and top up the water if it starts to
   low. Leave to stand for 10 minutes, then
   it out onto a plate and serve with cream

TOP TIP
Try serving the cake with brandy butter.

Dundee Cake

SERVES 10

PREPARATION TIME OVER NIGHT

COOKING TIME 1 HOUR 15 MINUTES

INGREDIENTS

- g / 12 oz / 1 ¾ cups mixed dried fruit
- g / 2 oz / ¼ cup glacé cherries, quartered
- ml / 2 fl. oz / ¼ cup whisky
- g / 4 oz / ½ cup butter, softened
- tsp treacle
- g / 4 oz / ½ cup dark brown sugar
- large eggs, beaten
- g / 2 oz / ⅓ cup self-raising flour
- tsp mixed spice
- tbsp ground almonds
- Brazil nuts, walnuts and macadamia nuts to decorate
- tbsp marmalade
- tbsp whisky

METHOD

1. Mix the dried fruit and cherries together and pour over the whisky. Leave to macerate overnight.

2. Preheat the oven to 150°C (130°C fan) / 300F / gas 2 and grease and line a 20 cm (8 in) square cake tin with greaseproof paper.

3. Cream the butter, treacle and sugar together until well whipped, then gradually whisk in the eggs, beating well after each addition. Sift over the flour and spice and fold it in with the ground almonds and dried fruit.

4. Scrape the mixture into the tin and arrange the nuts on top. Bake for 1 hour 15 minutes or until a skewer inserted in the centre comes out clean. Turn the loaf out onto a wire rack and leave to cool.

5. Heat the marmalade and whisky together, then pass it through a sieve to remove the peel and brush it over the top of the cake to glaze.

TOP TIP

Top the cake with a mixture of glacé cherries as well as the nuts.

125

Glazed Raspberry Financiers

MAKES 12

PREPARATION TIME 1 HOUR 30 MINUTES

COOKING TIME 10–15 MINUTES

INGREDIENTS

110 g / 4 oz / ½ cup butter
55 g / 2 oz / ⅓ cup plain (all-purpose) flour
55 g / 2 oz / ½ cup ground almonds
110 g / 4 oz / 1 cup icing (confectioners') sugar
3 large egg whites
100 g / 3 ½ oz / ⅔ cup raspberries
100 g / 1 ¾ oz / ½ cup raspberry jelly cubes

METHOD

1. Preheat the oven to 170°C (150°C fan) / 325F / gas 3 and oil and flour a 12-hole financier mould.

2. Heat the butter until it foams and starts to smell nutty, then leave to cool. Combine the flour, ground almonds and icing sugar in a bowl and whisk in the egg whites. Pour the cooled butter through a sieve into the bowl and whisk into the mixture until evenly mixed.

3. Spoon the mixture into the moulds and press a few raspberries into each one, then transfer the tin to the oven and bake for 10–15 minutes. Test with a wooden toothpick, if it comes out clean, the cakes are done. Transfer the cakes to a wire rack and leave to cool.

4. Make up the jelly according to the packet instructions, using half the recommended amount of water. Leave to cool at room temperature until it just starts to gel, then spoon the mixture onto the cakes to glaze.

TOP TIP
Try serving the financiers with white chocolate ice cream.

emon
ponge Cake

ES 8

ARATION TIME **15 MINUTES**

ING TIME **40 MINUTES**

REDIENTS

/ 6 oz / 1 ¼ cups self-raising flour, sifted

baking powder

/ 6 oz / ¾ cup caster (superfine) sugar

/ 6 oz / ¾ cup butter, softened

ge eggs

ons, zest finely grated

METHOD

1. Preheat the oven to 180°C (160°C fan) / 350F / gas 4 and oil and line a 23 cm (9 in) round cake tin with greaseproof paper.

2. Combine the flour, baking powder, sugar, butter, eggs and lemon zest in a bowl and whisk together for 2 minutes or until smooth.

3. Scrape the mixture into the tin and level the top, then bake for 40 minutes or until a toothpick inserted in the centre comes out clean. Turn the cake out onto a wire rack and leave to cool completely.

TOP TIP

Serve the cake warm drizzled with lemon curd and scoops of vanilla ice cream.

Fruit and Almond Loaf Cake

SERVES 8

PREPARATION TIME 15 MINUTES

COOKING TIME 55 MINUTES

INGREDIENTS

225 g / 8 oz / 1 ½ cups self-raising flour
100 g / 3 ½ oz / ½ cup butter, cubed
85 g / 3 oz / ⅓ cup caster (superfine) sugar
150 g / 5 ½ oz / ¾ cup mixed dried fruit
1 large egg
75 ml / 2 ½ fl. oz / ⅓ cup whole milk
75 g / 2 ½ oz / 1 cup blanched almonds

METHOD

1. Preheat the oven to 180°C (160°C fan) / 355F / gas 4 and line a loaf tin with greaseproof paper.

2. Sieve the flour into a mixing bowl and rub in the butter until it resembles fine breadcrumbs, then stir in the sugar and dried fruit. Lightly beat the egg with the milk and stir it into the dry ingredients until just combined.

3. Scrape the mixture into the loaf tin and sprinkle over the almonds, then bake for 55 minutes or until a skewer inserted in the centre comes out clean. Transfer the cake to a wire rack and leave to cool completely.

TOP TIP
Try glazing the cake with warm marmalade for a glossy finish.

Decorated Marble Loaf Cake

RVES 8

EPARATION TIME **30 MINUTES**

OKING TIME **45–50 MINUTES**

GREDIENTS

0 g / 3 ½ oz / ⅔ cup self-raising flour

sp baking powder

g / 1 ¾ oz / ½ cup ground almonds

0 g / 5 ½ oz / ⅔ cup caster (superfine) sugar

0 g / 5 ½ oz / ⅔ cup butter, softened

arge eggs

osp unsweetened cocoa powder

r the topping

0 ml / 7 fl. oz / ¾ cup double (heavy) cream

0 g / 7 oz / 1 ¼ cups dark chocolate, minimum
   60% cocoa solids, chopped

ocolate balls, cornflakes and chocolate
   cornflakes to decorate

METHOD

1. Preheat the oven to 180°C (160°C fan) / 350F / gas 4 and grease and line a loaf tin with greaseproof paper.

2. Sieve the flour and baking powder into a mixing bowl, then add the ground almonds, sugar, butter and eggs and whisk with an electric whisk for 4 minutes or until pale and well whipped.

3. Divide the mixture into 2 bowls. Mix the cocoa powder with 2 tbsp hot water until smooth and stir it into one of the bowls. Spoon the mixtures into the tin, alternating between chocolate and plain, then draw a knife through the middle to marble.

4. Bake for 45–50 minutes. Insert a toothpick into the centre, if it comes out clean the cake is done. Transfer the cake to a wire rack to cool completely.

5. Heat the cream until it starts to simmer, then pour it over the chopped chocolate and stir until smooth. Leave to thicken a little, then spoon it over the cake and top with chocolate balls, cornflakes and chocolate cornflakes before serving.

TOP TIP

Try adding the finely grated zest of an orange to the plain cake mixture.

Black Forest Gateau

SERVES 10

PREPARATION TIME 1 HOUR

COOKING TIME 25–30 MINUTES

INGREDIENTS

200 g / 7 oz / 1 ⅓ cups self-raising flour
200 g / 7 oz / ¾ cup caster (superfine) sugar
200 g / 7 oz / ¾ cup butter
4 large eggs
1 tsp baking powder
3 tbsp unsweetened cocoa powder

For the filling

250 g / 9 oz / 1 ⅔ cups black cherries, stoned
4 tbsp caster (superfine) sugar
2 tbsp kirsch
300 g / 10 ½ fl. oz / 1 ¼ cups double (heavy) cream

For the topping

200 ml / 7 fl. oz / ¾ cup double (heavy) cream
200 g / 7 oz / 1 ¼ cups dark chocolate,
    minimum 60% cocoa solids, chopped
2 tbsp chocolate flakes
3 whole cherries, stalks intact
2 tbsp icing (confectioners') sugar,
    plus extra for dusting

METHOD

1. Preheat the oven to 180°C (160°C fan) / 350F / gas 4 and grease and line two 20 cm (8 in) round loose-bottomed cake tins.

2. Put all of the cake ingredients in a large mixing bowl and whisk with an electric whisk for 4 minutes or until pale and well whipped. Divide the mixture between the tins and level the tops with a spatula, then bake for 25–30 minutes. The cakes are ready when a toothpick inserted in the centre comes out clean. Leave to cool completely.

3. Put the cherries in a saucepan with the sugar and kirsch, then cover and cook for 10 minutes or until soft. Leave to cool.

4. Whip the cream until it holds its shape. Strain the cherries and brush the juice over the cakes. Spread half of the cream on top of one of the cakes and top with the cherries. Top with the other cake and coat the top and sides with the rest of the cream.

5. Heat the cream to simmering point, then pour it over the chocolate. After 30 seconds stir until smoothly combined. Pour over the cake, allowing it to drip down the sides. Sprinkle with chocolate flakes.

6. Stir a few drops of water into the icing sugar to make a pourable icing, then dip in the cherries. Transfer to the top of the cake and leave to set. Dust the cake with icing sugar just before serving.

hocolate
ponge Cake

VES 8

PARATION TIME 20 MINUTES

KING TIME 35 MINUTES

REDIENTS

g / 6 oz / 1 ¼ cups self-raising flour
g / 6 oz / ¾ cup caster (superfine) sugar
g / 6 oz / ¾ cup butter, softened
ge eggs
baking powder
sp unsweetened cocoa powder
spberries, plus extra to serve
g (confectioners') sugar for dusting

METHOD

1. Preheat the oven to 180°C (160°C fan) / 350F / gas 4 and grease and line a 23 cm (9 in) round loose-bottomed cake tin.

2. Put the flour, sugar, butter, eggs, baking powder and cocoa in a large mixing bowl and whisk with an electric whisk for 4 minutes or until pale and well whipped.

3. Scrape the mixture into the tin and level the top with a spatula. Bake for 35 minutes or until a toothpick inserted in the centre comes out clean. Transfer the cake to a wire rack and leave to cool completely.

4. Arrange the raspberries on top of the cake and dust lightly with icing sugar.

TOP TIP

Try drizzling the finished cake with melted white chocolate.

Biscuits and Cookies

Almond Biscuits

MAKES 36

PREPARATION TIME 1 HOUR

COOKING TIME 15 MINUTES

INGREDIENTS

75 g / 2 ½ oz / ⅓ cup caster (superfine) sugar
175 g / 6 oz / ¾ cup butter, softened
150 g / 5 ½ oz / 1 cup plain (all-purpose) flour
150 g / 5 ½ oz / 1 ½ cups ground almonds

METHOD

1. Cream together the sugar and butter until pale and well whipped, then stir in the flour and ground almonds. Bring the mixture together into a ball with your ha then wrap in cling film and refrigerate f 45 minutes.

2. Preheat the oven to 140°C (120°C fan) / 275F / gas 1 and line two baking trays with greaseproof paper.

3. Divide the dough into 36 evenly sized ba then flatten them onto the prepared tray

4. Bake the biscuits for 25 minutes or until cooked through and golden. Transfer th biscuits to a wire rack and leave to cool completely.

TOP TIP

Try using ground pistachio nuts or hazelnuts (cobnuts) instead.

inger Nuts

ES 36

PARATION TIME **10 MINUTES**

KING TIME **15 MINUTES**

REDIENTS

- / 2 ½ oz / ⅓ cup butter, softened
- ₃ / 3 ½ oz / ⅓ cup golden syrup
- ₃ / 8 oz / 1 ½ cups self-raising flour
- ₃ / 3 ½ oz / ½ cup caster (superfine) sugar
- ● ground ginger
- ge egg, beaten

METHOD

1. Preheat the oven to 180°C (160°C fan) / 355F / gas 4 and line 2 baking trays with greaseproof paper.

2. Melt the butter and golden syrup together in a saucepan. Mix the flour, sugar and ground ginger together, then stir in the melted butter mixture and the beaten egg.

3. Use a teaspoon to portion the mixture onto the baking trays, leaving plenty of room for the biscuits to spread.

4. Bake for 15 minutes or until golden brown. Transfer the biscuits to a wire rack and leave to cool and harden.

TOP TIP

Add different spices to the biscuits such as ground cinnamon or nutmeg.

Sugar Nib Shortbread

MAKES 16

PREPARATION TIME 20 MINUTES

COOKING TIME 15–20 MINUTES

INGREDIENTS

225 g / 8 oz / 1 ½ cups plain (all-purpose) flour
75 g / 2 ½ oz / ⅓ cup caster (superfine) sugar
150 g / 5 oz / ⅔ cup butter, cubed
50 g / 1 ¾ oz / ¼ cup sugar nibs

METHOD

1. Preheat the oven to 180°C (160°C fan) / 355F / gas 4 and line a baking tray with greaseproof paper.

2. Mix together the flour and caster sugar a bowl, then rub in the butter. Knead gen until the mixture forms a smooth dough form into a cylinder 6 cm (2 ½ in) in diam

3. Slice the roll into 1 cm (½ in) thick slices and spread them out on the baking tray, sprinkle over the sugar nibs and press d lightly to secure.

4. Bake the biscuits for 15–20 minutes, tur the tray round halfway through. Transfe biscuits to a wire rack and leave to cool.

TOP TIP
Serve the shortbread with fruit fools for a great texture contrast.

Pecan Snap Biscuits

MAKES 36

PREPARATION TIME 10 MINUTES

COOKING TIME 10–12 MINUTES

INGREDIENTS

75 g / 2 ½ oz / ⅓ cup butter, softened
100 g / 3 ½ oz / ⅓ cup golden syrup
200 g / 8 oz / 1 ½ cups self-raising flour
100 g / 3 ½ oz / ½ cup caster (superfine) sugar
75 g / 2 ½ oz / ⅔ cup pecan nuts, finely chopped
1 large egg, beaten

METHOD

1. Preheat the oven to 180°C (160°C fan) / 3550F / gas 4 and line 2 baking trays with greaseproof paper.

2. Melt the butter and golden syrup together in a saucepan.

3. Mix the flour, sugar and pecans together, then stir in the melted butter mixture and the beaten egg.

4. Use a teaspoon to portion the mixture onto the baking trays, leaving plenty of room for the biscuits to spread.

5. Bake in batches for 12–15 minutes or until golden brown.

6. Transfer the biscuits to a wire rack and leave to cool and harden.

TOP TIP
Substitute the pecans for finely chopped hazelnuts (cobnuts).

Sponge Finger Biscuits

MAKES 45–50

PREPARATION TIME 20 MINUTES

COOKING TIME 10–15 MINUTES

INGREDIENTS

4 large eggs
125 g / 4 ½ oz / ½ cup caster (superfine) sugar
1 tsp vanilla extract
a pinch cream of tartar
110 g / 4 oz / ⅔ cup plain (all-purpose) flour
icing (confectioners') sugar for dusting

METHOD

1. Preheat the oven to 190°C (170°C fan) / 375F / gas 5 and grease and line 2 large baking trays with greaseproof paper.

2. Separate the eggs and put the yolks in a bowl with half of the sugar and the vanilla extract. Whisk for 4 minutes or until very thick and pale.

3. Whisk the egg whites with the cream of tartar, making sure the whisk and bowl are completely clean and grease-free. At the soft peak stage, gradually whisk in the remaining sugar.

4. Sieve the flour over the egg yolk mixture and scrape in the egg whites, then carefu fold it all together with a large metal spoo retaining as much air as possible.

5. Spoon the mixture into a piping bag fitted with a large plain nozzle. Pipe 10 cm (4 in) lines onto the baking trays, leaving room for the biscuits to spread. Bake the biscui for 10–15 minutes or until firm to the touc

6. Transfer to a wire rack and leave to cool completely then dust liberally with icing sugar.

TOP TIP
Use these sponge fingers to make tiramisu and trifles.

ugared astry iamonds

...KES **36**

...PARATION TIME **45 MINUTES**

...KING TIME **10 MINUTES**

...GREDIENTS

...g / 3 ½ oz / ½ cup butter, cubed and chilled
...g / 7 oz / 1 ⅓ cups plain (all-purpose) flour
...g, beaten
...sp granulated sugar

METHOD

1. Rub the butter into the flour until the mixture resembles fine breadcrumbs. Stir in just enough cold water to bring the pastry together into a pliable dough, then chill for 30 minutes.

2. Preheat the oven to 200°C (180°C fan) / 390F / gas 6.

3. Roll out the pastry on a floured surface, then brush the surface with egg and sprinkle with sugar. Use a fluted pastry wheel to cut the sheet into diamonds, then transfer them to a non-stick baking tray.

4. Bake the pastry for 10 minutes or until golden brown and crisp. Transfer to a wire rack and leave to cool before serving.

TOP TIP
Serve the diamonds with fruit fool for a great texture combination.

BISCUITS AND COOKIES

Chocolate Chip Cookies

MAKES **36**

PREPARATION TIME **10 MINUTES**

COOKING TIME **15 MINUTES**

INGREDIENTS

225 g / 8 oz / 1 ⅓ cups light brown sugar
100 g / 3 ½ oz / ½ cup caster (superfine) sugar
175 g / 6 oz / ¾ cup butter, melted
2 tsp vanilla extract
1 egg, plus 1 egg yolk
250 g / 9 oz / 1 ⅔ cups self-raising flour
100 g / 3 ½ oz / ⅔ cup milk chocolate chips

METHOD

1. Preheat the oven to 160°C (140°C fan) / 325F / gas 3 and line 2 baking trays with greaseproof paper.

2. Cream together the two sugars, butter and vanilla extract until pale and well whipped, then beat in the egg and yolk, followed by the flour and chocolate chips.

3. Drop tablespoons of the mixture onto the prepared trays, leaving plenty of room to spread.

4. Bake the cookies in batches for 15 minutes or until the edges are starting to brown, but the centres are still chewy. Transfer to a wire rack and leave to cool.

TOP TIP
Try using a mixture of white and dark chocolate chips for variety.

152

hocolate Chip
hortbread

ES 16

PARATION TIME 20 MINUTES

KING TIME 15–20 MINUTES

REDIENTS

g / 8 oz / 1 ½ cups plain (all-purpose) flour
/ 2 ½ oz / ⅓ cup caster (superfine) sugar
g / 5 oz / ⅔ cup butter, cubed
/ 1 ¾ oz / ¼ cup chocolate chips
sp unsweetened cocoa powder

METHOD

1. Preheat the oven to 180°C (160°C fan) / 355F / gas 4 and line a baking tray with greaseproof paper.

2. Mix together the flour and caster sugar in a bowl, then rub in the butter. Knead gently with the chocolate chips until the mixture forms a smooth dough, then form into a cylinder 6 cm (2 ⅓ in) in diameter.

3. Roll the cylinder in cocoa, then cut the roll into 1 cm (½ in) thick slices and spread them out on the baking tray.

4. Bake the biscuits for 15–20 minutes, turning the tray round halfway through. Transfer the biscuits to a wire rack and leave to cool.

TOP TIP

Sandwich the biscuits together in pairs with chocolate ice cream.

Glazed Lemon Madeleines

MAKES 12

PREPARATION TIME 1 HOUR 45 MINUTES

COOKING TIME 10–15 MINUTES

INGREDIENTS

110 g / 4 oz / ½ cup butter
55 g / 2 oz / ⅓ cup plain (all-purpose) flour
1 lemon, zest finely grated
55 g / 2 oz / ½ cup ground almonds
110 g / 4 oz / 1 cup icing (confectioners') sugar
3 large egg whites

For the glaze

1 lemon, juiced
110 g / 4 oz / 1 cup icing (confectioners') sugar

METHOD

1. Heat the butter until it foams and starts to smell nutty, then leave to cool.

2. Combine the flour, lemon zest, ground almonds and icing sugar in a bowl and whisk in the egg whites. Pour the cooled butter through a sieve into the bowl and whisk into the mixture until evenly mixed. Leave the cake mixture to rest in the fridge for 1 hour.

3. Preheat the oven to 170°C (150°C fan) / 325F / gas 3 and oil and flour a 12-hole madeleine mould.

4. Spoon the mixture into the moulds, then transfer the tin to the oven and bake for 10–15 minutes. Test with a wooden toothpick, if it comes out clean, the cakes are done. Transfer the cakes to a wire rack to cool.

5. To make the glaze, stir the lemon juice into the icing sugar a little at a time until it forms a pourable icing. Dip the madeleines in the icing to coat, then leave to dry and set on a wire rack.

TOP TIP
Try serving these little cakes with lemon mousse.

hocolate and razil Nut ookies

ES 36

PARATION TIME **30 MINUTES**

KING TIME **15 MINUTES**

REDIENTS

g / 8 oz / 1 ⅓ cups light brown sugar
g / 3 ½ oz / ½ cup caster (superfine) sugar
g / 6 oz / ¾ cup butter, melted
vanilla extract
g, plus 1 egg yolk
g / 9 oz / 1 ⅔ cups self-raising flour
g / 3 ½ oz / ⅔ cup milk chocolate chips
/ 1 ¾ oz / ½ cup Brazil nuts, chopped
g / 3 ½ oz milk chocolate, broken into squares

METHOD

1. Preheat the oven to 160°C (140°C fan) / 325F / gas 3 and line 2 baking trays with greaseproof paper.

2. Cream together the two sugars, butter and vanilla extract until pale and well whipped, then beat in the egg and yolk, followed by the flour, chocolate chips and Brazil nuts.

3. Drop tablespoons of the mixture onto the prepared trays, leaving plenty of room to spread.

4. Bake the cookies in batches for 15 minutes or until the edges are starting to brown, but the centres are still chewy. Transfer to a wire rack and leave to cool.

5. Melt the chocolate in a microwave or bain marie, then dip the underside of each biscuit and leave to set on greaseproof paper.

TOP TIP
Serve the cookies with mugs of hot chocolate.

Chocolate Chip and Almond Cookies

MAKES 36

PREPARATION TIME 10 MINUTES

COOKING TIME 15 MINUTES

INGREDIENTS

225 g / 8 oz / 1 ⅓ cups light brown sugar
100 g / 3 ½ oz / ½ cup caster (superfine) sugar
175 g / 6 oz / ¾ cup butter, melted
1 tsp almond extract
1 egg, plus 1 egg yolk
250 g / 9 oz / 1 ⅔ cups self-raising flour
50 g / 1 ¾ oz / ⅔ cup flaked (slivered) almonds, chopped
100 g / 3 ½ oz / ⅔ cup milk chocolate chips

METHOD

1. Preheat the oven to 160°C (140°C fan) / 325F / gas 3 and line 2 baking trays with greaseproof paper.

2. Cream together the two sugars, butter and almond extract until pale and well whipped, then beat in the egg and yolk, followed by the flour, almonds and chocolate chips.

3. Drop tablespoons of the mixture onto the prepared trays, leaving plenty of room to spread.

4. Bake the cookies in batches for 15 minutes or until the edges are starting to brown, but the centres are still chewy. Transfer to a wire rack and leave to cool.

TOP TIP

Try replacing the almonds with pistachio nuts.

am Flower Biscuits

MAKES 36

PREPARATION TIME 1 HOUR 15 MINUTES

BAKING TIME 25 MINUTES

INGREDIENTS

g / 5 ½ oz / ⅔ cup caster (superfine) sugar

g / 12 oz / 1 ½ cups butter, softened

vanilla extract

g / 10 ½ oz / 2 cups plain (all-purpose) flour

g / 5 ½ oz / 1 ½ cups ground almonds

g / 4 ½ oz / ½ cup strawberry jam (jelly)

g / 4 ½ oz / ½ cup apricot jam (jelly)

METHOD

1. Cream together the sugar, butter and vanilla extract until pale and well whipped, then stir in the flour and ground almonds. Bring the mixture together into a ball with your hands, then wrap in cling film and refrigerate for 45 minutes.

2. Preheat the oven to 140°C (120°C fan) / 275F / gas 1 and line 2 baking trays with greaseproof paper.

3. Roll out the dough on a lightly floured surface to 5 mm (¼ in) thickness. Use a flower-shaped pastry cutter to cut out 72 biscuits, re-rolling the trimmings as necessary. Use a small round cutter to cut out the centre of 36 of the biscuits.

4. Transfer the biscuits to the prepared trays and bake in batches for 25 minutes or until cooked through and golden. Transfer the biscuits to a wire rack and leave to cool.

5. Sandwich the plain biscuits and centre-less biscuits together in pairs with the jam.

TOP TIP

Try replacing the jam with chocolate and hazelnut (cobnut) spread.

163

Peppermint Sponge Fingers

MAKES 40–50

PREPARATION TIME 20 MINUTES

COOKING TIME 10–15 MINUTES

INGREDIENTS

4 large eggs
125 g / 4 ½ oz / ½ cup caster (superfine) sugar
a few drops of peppermint essence
a pinch cream of tartar
110 g / 4 oz / ⅔ cup plain (all-purpose) flour
icing (confectioners') sugar for dusting
mint-choc-chip ice cream and peppermint tea
    to serve

METHOD

1. Preheat the oven to 190°C (170°C fan) / 375F / gas 5 and grease and line 2 large baking trays with greaseproof paper.

2. Separate the eggs and put the yolks in a bowl with half of the sugar and the peppermint essence. Whisk for 4 minutes or until very thick and pale.

3. Whisk the egg whites with the cream of tartar, making sure the whisk and bowl completely clean and grease-free. At the soft peak stage, gradually whisk in the remaining sugar.

4. Sieve the flour over the egg yolk mixture and scrape in the egg whites, then carefully fold it all together, retaining as much air as possible.

5. Spoon the mixture into a piping bag fitted with a large plain nozzle. Pipe 10 cm (4 in) lines onto the baking trays, leaving room for the biscuits to spread. Bake the biscuits for 10–15 minutes or until firm to the touch.

6. Transfer to a wire rack and leave to cool completely then dust liberally with icing sugar. Serve with mint-choc-chip ice cream and peppermint tea.

TOP TIP

Try serving the sponge fingers with chocolate mousse.

Double Choc and Nut Cookies

MAKES 36

PREPARATION TIME 30 MINUTES

COOKING TIME 15 MINUTES

INGREDIENTS

- 5 g / 8 oz / 1 ⅔ cups light brown sugar
- g / 3 ½ oz / ½ cup caster (superfine) sugar
- g / 6 oz / ¾ cup butter, melted
- sp vanilla extract
- gg, plus 1 egg yolk
- 0 g / 7 oz / 1 ⅓ cups self-raising flour
- g / ⅓ oz / ½ cup unsweetened cocoa powder
- g / 3 ½ oz / ⅔ cup dark chocolate chips
- g / 1 ¾ oz / ½ cup peanuts, chopped

METHOD

1. Preheat the oven to 160°C (140°C fan) / 325F / gas 3 and line 2 baking trays with greaseproof paper.

2. Cream together the two sugars, butter and vanilla extract until pale and well whipped, then beat in the egg and yolk, followed by the flour, cocoa, chocolate chips and peanuts.

3. Drop tablespoons of the mixture onto the prepared trays, leaving plenty of room to spread.

4. Bake the cookies in batches for 15 minutes or until the edges are starting to brown, but the centres are still chewy. Transfer to a wire rack and leave to cool.

TOP TIP

Try sandwiching the cookies together with mint-choc-chip ice cream.

Chocolate Sandwich Biscuits

MAKES 24

PREPARATION TIME 1 HOUR 15 MINUTES

COOKING TIME 25 MINUTES

INGREDIENTS

150 g / 5 ½ oz / ⅔ cup caster (superfine) sugar
350 g / 12 oz / 1 ½ cups butter, softened
300 g / 10 ½ oz / 2 cups plain (all-purpose) flour
150 g / 5 ½ oz / 1 ½ cups ground almonds
150 g / 5 ½ oz / 1 cup dark chocolate (minimum 70% cocoa solids)

METHOD

1. Cream together the sugar and butter until pale and well whipped, then stir in the flou and ground almonds. Bring the mixture together into a ball with your hands, then wrap in cling film and refrigerate for 45 minutes.

2. Preheat the oven to 140°C (120°C fan) / 275F / gas 1 and line 2 baking trays with greaseproof paper.

3. Roll out the dough on a lightly floured surface to 5 mm (¼ in) thick. Use a round, fluted pastry cutter to cut out 48 biscuits, re-rolling the trimmings as necessary. Use a small, heart-shaped cutter to cut the centre out of 24 of the biscuits.

4. Transfer the biscuits to the prepared trays and bake in batches for 25 minutes or until cooked through and golden. Transfer the biscuits to a wire rack and leave to cool.

5. Melt the chocolate in a microwave or bain-marie, then use to sandwich the plain biscuits and centre-less biscuits together in pairs. Allow the chocolate to set before serving.

TOP TIP

Try replacing the melted chocolate with your favourite jam (jelly).

Demerara Meringues

MAKES 8

PREPARATION TIME 20 MINUTES

COOKING TIME 1 HOUR

INGREDIENTS

large egg whites

g / 4 oz / 1 cup caster (superfine) sugar

tbsp demerara sugar

METHOD

1. Preheat the oven to 140°C (120°C fan) / 275F / gas 1 and oil and line a large baking tray with greaseproof paper.

2. Whisk the egg whites until stiff, then gradually whisk in half the caster sugar until the mixture is very shiny. Fold in the remaining caster sugar with a large metal spoon, being careful to retain as much air as possible.

3. Spoon the meringue into a piping bag fitted with a large star nozzle and pipe 8 swirls onto the baking tray. Sprinkle the tops with demerara sugar, then transfer the tray to the oven and bake for 1 hour.

4. Turn off the oven and leave the meringues to cool slowly inside before serving.

TOP TIP

Dip the meringues in melted dark chocolate for a rich finish.

Raspberry Macaroons

MAKES 18

PREPARATION TIME 1 HOUR 15 MINUTES

COOKING TIME 10–15 MINUTES

INGREDIENTS

175 g / 6 oz / 1 ½ cups ground almonds
175 g / 6 oz / 1 ½ cups icing (confectioners') sugar
2 large egg whites
1 tbsp raspberry syrup
a few drops of pink food dye
110 g / 4 oz / ½ cup raspberry jam (jelly)

METHOD

1. Oil and line a large baking tray with greaseproof paper.

2. Grind the ground almonds and icing sugar together in a food processor to a very fine powder. Whisk the egg whites to stiff peak in a very clean bowl, then carefully fold in the almond and sugar mixture with the raspberry syrup and food dye.

3. Spoon the mixture into a piping bag fitted with a large plain nozzle and pipe 2.5 cm (1 in) rounds onto the baking tray. Leave the uncooked macaroons to stand for 30 minutes to form a skin.

4. Preheat the oven to 170°C (150°C fan) / 325F / gas 3.

5. Bake for 10–15 minutes or until crisp on the outside and still a bit chewy in the middle. Slide the greaseproof paper onto cold work surface and leave the macaroons to cool completely. Sandwich the macaroons together with jam.

TOP TIP
Add a few drops of rose water to the macaroon mixture.

Desserts

DESSERTS

Rhubarb Meringue Pie

MAKES 4

PREPARATION TIME 10–15 MINUTES

COOKING TIME 20–25 MINUTES

INGREDIENTS

250 g / 9 oz ready-made shortcrust pastry
a little plain (all-purpose) flour, for dusting
675 g / 1 lb 8 oz / 5 cups rhubarb,
    trimmed and sliced
75 g / 3 oz / ⅓ cup caster (superfine) sugar
60 ml / 2 fl. oz / ¼ cup cold water

For the meringue
2 medium egg whites
110 g / 4 oz / ½ cup caster (superfine) sugar
¼ tsp cream of tartar
a pinch of salt

METHOD

1. Preheat the oven to 180°C (160°C fan) / 350F / gas 4.

2. Roll the pastry out on a lightly floured surface to 5 mm (¼ in) thickness, then cut out 4 rounds of pastry and use to line 4 individual 12 cm (5 in) fluted tartlet cases.

3. Prick the bases with a fork and trim any excess, overhanging pastry.

4. Line with greaseproof paper and fill with baking beans, then blind bake for 12–15 minutes until golden at the edges.

5. Remove from the oven, discard the greaseproof paper and baking beans, then return to the oven for 3–4 minutes to brown the base. Remove to a wire rack to cool.

6. Combine the rhubarb, sugar and water in a saucepan and cook over a medium heat, covered, until soft. Drain and allow to cool.

7. Whisk the egg whites with the salt in a large clean mixing bowl until soft peaks form.

8. Add the cream of tartar and sugar, 1 tbsp at a time, beating well between additions until you have a thick, glossy meringue. Spoon into a piping bag fitted with a 2 cm (1 in) star-shaped nozzle.

9. Increase the oven to 220°C (200°C fan) / 425F / gas 7. Fill the pastry with the rhubarb and pipe the meringue on top in blobs.

10. Bake for 8–10 minutes until the meringue is browned, then remove from the oven. Dust with icing sugar before serving.

Summer Fruit Crumble

SERVES 4

PREPARATION TIME 10 MINUTES

COOKING TIME 40 MINUTES

INGREDIENTS

300 g / 10 ½ oz / 2 cups mixed summer fruit

2 tbsp caster (superfine) sugar

75 g / 2 ½ oz / ⅓ cup butter

50 g / 1 ¾ oz / ⅓ cup plain (all-purpose) flour

25 g / 1 oz / ½ cup ground almonds

40 g / 1 ½ oz / ¼ cup light brown sugar

METHOD

1. Preheat the oven to 180°C (160°C fan) / 355F / gas 4.

2. Mix the fruit with the caster sugar and tip it into a baking dish.

3. Rub the butter into the flour and stir in the ground almonds and brown sugar. Take a handful of the topping and squeeze it into a clump, then crumble it over the fruit.

4. Repeat with the rest of the crumble mixture, then bake for 40 minutes or until the topping is golden brown.

TOP TIP

Try spicing the crumble topping with 2 tsp of ground cinnamon.

Lemon Curd Tart

SERVES 8

PREPARATION TIME 55 MINUTES

COOKING TIME 15–20 MINUTES

INGREDIENTS

2 tsp cornflour (cornstarch)
4 lemons, zested and juiced
4 large eggs, beaten
225 g / 8 oz / 1 cup butter
175 g / 6 oz / ¾ cup caster (superfine) sugar

For the pastry

100 g / 3 ½ oz / ½ cup butter, cubed
200 g / 7 oz / 1 ⅓ cups plain (all-purpose) flour
55 g / 2 oz / ½ cup caster (superfine) sugar
1 egg, beaten

To decorate

1 lemon, zest finely pared
2 slices lemon

METHOD

1. Preheat the oven to 200°C (180°C fan) / 390F / gas 6.

2. To make the pastry, rub the butter into the flour and sugar, then add the egg with just enough cold water to bind. Wrap the dough in cling film and chill for 30 minutes, then roll out on a floured surface.

3. Use the pastry to line a 23 cm (9 in) loose-bottomed tart tin and trim the edges. Prick the pastry with a fork, line with cling film and fill with baking beans. Bake for 10 minutes, then remove the cling film and baking beans and cook for another 8 minutes to crisp.

4. Meanwhile, dissolve the cornflour in the lemon juice and put it in a saucepan with the rest of the ingredients. Stir constantly over medium heat to melt the butter and dissolve the sugar. After 6 or 7 minutes the mixture should thicken. Continue until it starts to bubble, then spoon it into the pastry case and level with a palette knife.

5. Leave to cool completely, then decorate with the lemon zest and slices.

TOP TIP
Sprinkle the top with sugar and caramelize with a blowtorch just before serving.

trawberry artlets

<ES 6

PARATION TIME **2 HOURS**

KING TIME **12 MINUTES**

GREDIENTS

g / 8 oz / 1 ½ cups plain (all-purpose) flour
g / 4 oz / ½ cup butter, cubed and chilled

the crème patissiere

ml / 9 fl. oz / 1 cup milk
rge egg yolks
/ 2 oz / ¼ cup caster (superfine) sugar
sp plain (all-purpose) flour
sp cornflour (cornstarch)
p vanilla extract

ecorate

g / 9 oz / 1 ⅔ cups strawberries, quartered
g (confectioners') sugar for dusting
t leaves to garnish

METHOD

1. Preheat the oven to 200°C (180°C fan) / 400F / gas 6.

2. Sieve the flour into a mixing bowl, then rub in the butter until the mixture resembles fine breadcrumbs. Stir in just enough cold water to bring the pastry together into a pliable dough.

3. Roll out the pastry on a floured surface and cut out 6 circles, then use them to line 6 tartlet tins. Line the tins with cling film and fill with baking beans, then bake for 10 minutes. Remove the film and beans and return the cases to the oven for 2 minutes or until cooked through. Leave to cool.

4. Heat the milk in a saucepan until just simmering. Meanwhile, whisk together the egg yolks, sugar, flours and vanilla in a heatproof bowl. Slowly pour on the milk, whisking all the time, then transfer back to the pan. Heat very gently, stirring until thickened. Spoon into the pastry cases and leave to cool.

5. Pile the strawberries on top of the tartlets and dust with icing sugar. Garnish with mint.

TOP TIP

Top these tarts with a variety of berries and sliced fruit and glaze with jam (jelly).

Blueberry Lattice Tartlets

MAKES 4

PREPARATION TIME 1 HOUR

COOKING TIME 25 MINUTES

INGREDIENTS

225 g / 8 oz / 1 ½ cups plain (all-purpose) flour
110 g / 4 oz / ½ cup butter, cubed and chilled
150 g / 5 ½ oz / 1 cup blueberries
225 g / 8 oz / 1 cup blueberry jam (jelly)
1 egg, beaten

METHOD

1. Preheat the oven to 200°C (180°C fan) / 400F / gas 6.

2. Sieve the flour into a mixing bowl, then rub in the butter until the mixture resembles fine breadcrumbs. Stir in just enough cold water to bring the pastry together into a pliable dough. Chill for 30 minutes.

3. Roll out the pastry on a floured surface and cut out 6 circles, then use them to line 6 tartlet tins. Re-roll the trimmings and cut the sheet into 1 cm (½ in) strips.

4. Mix the blueberries with the jam and spoon it into the pastry cases. Lay the pastry strips over the top in a lattice pattern and crimp the edges to seal. Brush the pastry with beaten egg.

5. Bake the tartlets for 25 minutes or until the pastry is cooked underneath and golden brown on top.

TOP TIP

These tarts work well with blackcurrants and 1 tbsp sugar, instead of blueberries.

pple, Almond nd Sultana trudel

VES 8

PARATION TIME 25 MINUTES

KING TIME 35–45 MINUTES

REDIENTS

- g / 8 oz / ¾ cup filo pastry
- g / 3 ½ oz / ½ cup butter, melted
- amley apples, peeled, cored and chopped
- g / 3 ½ oz / 1 cup ground almonds
- g / 3 ½ oz / ⅔ cup golden sultanas
- g / 3 ½ oz / ½ cup light brown sugar
- ground cinnamon
- p flaked (slivered) almonds
- (confectioners') sugar to dust

METHOD

1. Preheat the oven to 180°C (160°C fan) / 355F / gas 4 and grease a large baking tray.

2. Brush the filo pastry sheets with melted butter and lay the buttered sheets on top of one another on a sheet of cling film. Use at least 4 sheets of pastry.

3. Mix the apples with the ground almonds and sultanas and stir in the sugar and cinnamon. Spread the filling out along one edge of the pastry, then use the cling film to help you roll it up, tucking in the edges as you go.

4. Transfer the strudel to the baking tray, then brush with a little more melted butter and sprinkle with flaked almonds. Bake the strudel in the oven for 35–45 minutes or until the pastry is golden and crisp.

5. Dust the strudel with icing sugar and serve.

TOP TIP

Try replacing the apples with pears.

Cheesecake with Summer Fruit

SERVES 6

PREPARATION TIME 20 MINUTES

COOKING TIME 40 MINUTES

INGREDIENTS

100 g / 3 ½ oz / ½ cup digestive biscuits,
   crushed to crumbs
50 g / 1 ¾ oz / ¼ cup butter, melted
600 g / 1 lb / 2 cups cream cheese
2 tbsp plain (all-purpose) flour
125 g / 4 oz / ½ cup caster (superfine) sugar
1 ½ tsp vanilla extract
2 eggs
1 egg yolk
150 ml / 5 oz / ⅔ cup sour cream
500 g / 1 lb / 2 cups mixed summer fruit

METHOD

1. Preheat the oven to 180°C (160°C fan)
   / 350F / gas 5.

2. Stir the biscuits into the melted butter.
   Press into the bottom of a large
   springform cake tin.

3. Place on a baking tray and bake for
   5 minutes.

4. Whisk together the cheese, flour and
   sugar, then beat in the vanilla, eggs and
   sour cream until pale and smooth.

5. Spoon on top of the biscuit base and retu
   to the oven to bake for about 40 minutes.

6. Once the centre is set, remove from the
   oven and leave to cool. Decorate with
   fruit and serve.

TOP TIP
Add 2 tbsp maple syrup
to the mix for a smoky
sweetness.

ndividual
trawberry
avlovas

KES 4

EPARATION TIME **1 HOUR 30 MINUTES**

)KING TIME **1 HOUR**

GREDIENTS

rge egg whites

g / 4 oz / 1 cup caster (superfine) sugar

p cornflour (cornstarch)

ml / 8 fl. oz / 1 cup double (heavy) cream

sp icing (confectioners') sugar

sp vanilla extract

g / 5 ½ oz / 1 cup strawberries, halved

sp strawberry syrup

METHOD

1. Preheat the oven to 140°C (120°C fan) / 275F / gas 1 and oil and line a baking tray with greaseproof paper.

2. Whisk the egg whites until stiff, then gradually whisk in half the sugar until the mixture is very shiny. Fold in the remaining sugar and the cornflour, then spoon the mixture into 4 mounds on the baking tray.

3. Bake the meringues for 1 hour or until crisp on the outside, but still a bit chewy in the middle. Turn off the oven and leave to cool completely inside.

4. Whip the cream with the icing sugar and vanilla until it just holds its shape, then spoon it on top of the meringues. Arrange the strawberries on top and drizzle with strawberry syrup.

TOP TIP

Try peach slices and raspberry syrup for peach melba pavlovas.

Apricot Ripple Cheesecake

SERVES 8

PREPARATION TIME 4 HOURS

COOKING TIME 10 MINUTES

INGREDIENTS

12 apricots, halved and stoned
100 ml / 3 ½ fl. oz / ½ cup apple juice
4 tbsp runny honey
50 g / 1 ¾ oz / ¼ cup butter
200 g / 7 oz / ¾ cup digestive biscuits, crushed
150 g / 5 ½ oz / ⅔ cup cream cheese, well chilled
150 g / 5 ½ oz / ⅔ cup condensed milk,
    well chilled
2 lemons, juiced

METHOD

1. Put the apricots in a saucepan with the apple juice and honey. Cover and simmer gently for 8 minutes or until the apricots are soft, then remove from the pan with a slotted spoon and transfer to a liquidizer. Blend with enough of the cooking liquid to make a thick purée, then leave to cool.

2. Melt the butter and stir in the crushed biscuits, then tip the mixture into a rectangular baking dish and press down firmly into an even layer.

3. Beat the cream cheese with an electric and whisk until smooth, then whisk in the condensed milk. Whisk in the lemon juice until the mixture starts to thicken, then pour it onto the biscuit base and level the top.

4. Spoon dollops of the apricot purée over the top, then swirl the 2 together with a skewer. Chill in the fridge for at least 3 hours before serving.

TOP TIP
Add a few drops of orange flower water to the cheesecake mixture.

pple nd Thyme rangipane arts

KES 6

EPARATION TIME 20 MINUTES

OKING TIME 15–20 MINUTES

GREDIENTS

) g / 1 lb / 1 ½ cups ready-to-roll puff pastry
g / 2 ½ oz / ¾ cup ground almonds
g / 2 ½ oz / ⅓ cup butter, softened
g / 2 ½ oz / ⅓ cup caster (superfine) sugar
arge egg
bsp thyme leaves
bsp plain (all-purpose) flour
ating apples, cored and thinly sliced
me sprigs to garnish
ng (confectioners') sugar to dust

METHOD

1. Preheat the oven to 200°C (180°C fan) / 400F / gas 6.

2. Roll out the pastry on a floured surface and cut out 6 x 10 cm (4 in) circles, then transfer them to a greased baking tray.

3. Whisk together the almonds, butter, sugar, eggs, thyme and flour until well whipped and smooth, then spoon the mixture onto the pastry circles.

4. Arrange a few apple slices on top of each tart, then bake for 15–20 minutes or until the tops are golden brown and the pastry is crisp underneath.

5. Serve garnished with thyme and dusted with icing sugar.

TOP TIP

Try replacing the apples with slices of plum when they're in season.

DESSERTS

Mirabelle Clafoutis

SERVES 6

PREPARATION TIME 20 MINUTES

COOKING TIME 35–40 MINUTES

INGREDIENTS

75 g / 2 ½ oz / ⅓ cup butter
75 g / 2 ½ oz / ⅓ cup caster (superfine) sugar
300 ml / 10 ½ fl. oz / 1 ¼ cups whole milk
2 large eggs
50 g / 1 ¾ oz / ⅓ cup plain (all-purpose) flour
2 tbsp ground almonds
300 g / 10 ½ oz / 2 cups mirabelle plums
icing (confectioners') sugar for dusting

METHOD

1. Preheat the oven to 190°C (170°C fan) / 375F / gas 5.

2. Melt the butter in a saucepan and cook over a low heat until it starts to smell nutt Brush a little of the butter around the insi of a baking dish, then add a spoonful of the caster sugar and shake to coat.

3. Whisk together the milk and eggs with the rest of the butter. Sift the flour into a mixing bowl with a pinch of salt, then stir in the ground almonds and the rest of the sugar. Make a well in the middle of the dry ingredients and gradually whisk in the liquid, incorporating all the flour from rou the outside until you have a lump-free batt

4. Arrange the mirabelles in the baking dish and pour over the batter. Bake the clafouti for 35–45 minutes or until a skewer insert in the centre comes out clean. Dust with icing sugar and serve warm or cold.

TOP TIP
Try replacing the mirabelles with seedless grapes.

Summer Fruit Tartlets

MAKES 6

PREPARATION TIME 2 HOURS

COOKING TIME 12 MINUTES

INGREDIENTS

225 g / 8 oz / 1 ½ cups plain (all-purpose) flour
110 g / 4 oz / ½ cup butter, cubed and chilled

for the crème patissiere

4 large egg yolks
55 g / 2 oz / ¼ cup caster (superfine) sugar
2 tbsp plain (all-purpose) flour
2 tsp cornflour (cornstarch)
1 tsp vanilla extract
250 ml / 9 fl. oz / 1 cup whole milk

to decorate

6 strawberries, halved
6 cherries
12 raspberries
25 g (confectioners') sugar for dusting
mint leaves to garnish

METHOD

1. Preheat the oven to 200°C (180°C fan) / 400F / gas 6.

2. Sieve the flour into a mixing bowl, then rub in the butter until the mixture resembles fine breadcrumbs. Stir in just enough cold water to bring the pastry together into a pliable dough.

3. Heat the milk in a saucepan until just simmering. Meanwhile, whisk together the egg yolks, sugar, flours and vanilla in a heatproof bowl. Slowly pour on the milk, whisking all the time, then transfer back to the pan. Heat very gently, stirring until thickened. Spoon into the pastry cases and leave to cool.

4. To make the crème patissiere, stir the egg yolks, sugar, flours and vanilla extract together in a saucepan, then gradually add the milk. Heat the mixture until it starts to boil, stirring all the time, then take off the heat and beat vigorously to remove any lumps. Spoon the crème patissiere into the tartlet cases and leave to cool.

5. Arrange the strawberries, cherries and raspberries on top of the tartlets and dust with icing sugar. Garnish with mint.

TOP TIP
Add citrus to the crème patissiere with lemon zest instead of vanilla extract.

Pear Tarte Tatin

SERVES 6

PREPARATION TIME 10 MINUTES

COOKING TIME 40 MINUTES

INGREDIENTS

3 tbsp butter, softened and cubed
5–6 small pears, peeled, quartered and cored
2 star anise
4 tbsp soft light brown sugar
100 ml / 3 ½ fl. oz / ½ cup apple juice
300 g / 10 ½ oz / 1 cup all-butter puff pastry

METHOD

1. Preheat the oven to 220°C (200°C fan) / 425F / gas 7.

2. Melt the butter in a large frying pan, then fry the pears and star anise in a single la for 5 minutes or until they start to brown

3. Stir the sugar into the apple juice and pou it over the pears, then cook until the liqu has reduced to a syrupy glaze.

4. Arrange the pears in a small ovenproof frying pan and spoon over the cooking liqu

5. Roll out the pastry on a floured surface a cut out a circle the same diameter as the

6. Lay the pastry over the pears and tuck in edges, then transfer the tin to the oven a bake for 25 minutes or until the pastry is golden brown and cooked through.

7. Using oven gloves, put a large plate on to of the pan and turn them both over in one smooth movement to un-mould the tart.

TOP TIP

Top the tart with chopped honey-roasted almonds for added crunch.

oconut Tart

KES **12**

EPARATION TIME **15 MINUTES**

OKING TIME **20 MINUTES**

GREDIENTS

g / 3 ½ oz / ½ cup butter, cubed and chilled

g / 7 oz / 1 ⅔ cups plain (all-purpose) flour

g / 7 oz / ⅔ cup raspberry jam (jelly)

rge egg whites

g / 3 ½ oz / ½ cup caster (superfine) sugar

g / 9 oz / 1 ¼ cups unsweetened shredded coconut

g (confectioners') sugar for dusting

METHOD

1. Preheat the oven to 200°C (180°C fan) / 400F / gas 6.

2. Rub the butter into the flour until the mixture resembles fine breadcrumbs. Stir in just enough cold water to bring the pastry together into a pliable dough, then chill for 30 minutes.

3. Roll out the pastry on a floured surface and use it to line a greased Swiss roll tin. Spread the jam on top.

4. Whisk the egg whites to stiff peaks in a very clean bowl, then fold in the sugar and the coconut.

5. Spoon the mixture into a piping bag fitted with a large star nozzle and pipe it over the surface in an even layer.

6. Bake the tart for 30 minutes or until the pastry is cooked underneath and the coconut topping is golden brown. Leave to cool completely then cut it into 12 squares and dust with icing sugar.

TOP TIP

Try replacing the jam with chocolate and hazelnut (cobnut) spread.

Lemon Domed Biscuits

MAKES 6

PREPARATION TIME **1 HOUR 15 MINUTES**

COOKING TIME **20–25 MINUTES**

INGREDIENTS

125 g / 4 ½ oz / ½ cup butter, cubed
125 g / 4 ½ oz / ¾ cup plain (all-purpose) flour
125 g / 4 ½ oz / ½ cup caster (superfine) sugar
3 large egg yolks, beaten

For the lemon domes

2 tsp cornflour (cornstarch)
4 lemons, zested and juiced
4 large eggs, beaten
225 g / 8 oz / 1 cup butter
175 g / 6 oz / ¾ cup caster (superfine) sugar
4 tbsp icing (confectioners') sugar

METHOD

1. Preheat the oven to 180°C (160°C fan) / 350F / gas 4 and line a baking tray with greaseproof paper.

2. Rub the butter into the flour with a pinch of salt, then stir in the sugar, then the egg yolks. Bring the mixture together into a s dough and roll it out between 2 sheets of greaseproof paper until 2 cm (¾ in) thick.

3. Use a cookie cutter to cut out 6 biscuits a transfer them to a baking tray. Bake the biscuits for 20–25 minutes or until golden brown. Transfer the biscuits to a wire rac and leave to cool.

4. Meanwhile, dissolve the cornflour in the lemon juice and put it in a saucepan with the rest of the ingredients except the icin sugar. Stir over a medium heat; after 6 or 7 minutes the mixture should thicken. Continue until it starts to bubble, then spoon it into a 6-hole silicone half-sphere mould. Leave to cool, then chill in the frid until set.

5. Stir cold water into the icing sugar a few drops at a time until you have a thick icing Spoon it into a piping bag, fitted with a sm plain nozzle. Turn each lemon dome out o a biscuit and drizzle a little icing over the t

TOP TIP
Serve the biscuits with lemon sorbet.

hocolate nd Walnut ondants

KES 6

EPARATION TIME 50 MINUTES

OKING TIME 8 MINUTES

GREDIENTS

- sp walnuts, finely chopped
- sp demerara sugar
- g / 6 oz / ¾ cup dark chocolate, minimum 60% cocoa solids, chopped
- g / 6 oz / ²⁄₃ cup butter, chopped
- g / 3 oz / ⅓ cup caster (superfine) sugar
- rge eggs, plus 3 egg yolks
- sp plain (all-purpose) flour
- sp unsweetened cocoa powder

METHOD

1. Mix the walnuts and demerara sugar together. Oil the inside of 6 mini pudding basins, then spoon in the walnut mixture and shake to coat.

2. Melt the chocolate, butter and caster sugar together in a saucepan, stirring to dissolve the sugar. Leave to cool a little, then beat in the eggs and egg yolks and fold in the flour. Divide the mixture between the pudding basins, then chill for 30 minutes.

3. Preheat the oven to 180°C (160°C fan) / 350F / gas 4 and put a baking tray in to heat. Transfer the fondants to the heated baking tray and bake in the oven for 8 minutes.

4. Leave the fondants to cool for 2 minutes, then dust with the cocoa powder and serve.

TOP TIP
Try replacing the chopped walnuts with chopped hazelnuts (cobnuts).

Coconut Soufflés

MAKES **4**

PREPARATION TIME **25 MINUTES**

COOKING TIME **15–20 MINUTES**

INGREDIENTS

3 tbsp desiccated coconut
4 tbsp coconut liqueur
1 tbsp butter, melted
75 g / 2 ½ oz / ⅓ cup caster (superfine) sugar
5 large egg whites
icing (confectioners') sugar for dusting

METHOD

1. Preheat the oven to 170°C (150°C fan) / 325F / gas 3 and put a kettle of water on to boil.

2. Combine the desiccated coconut and coconut liqueur in a bowl and leave to soften while you prepare the soufflé base.

3. Brush 4 large glass ramekins with butter then sprinkle the insides with 1 tbsp of the caster sugar.

4. Whip the egg whites until they form stiff peaks, then gradually whisk in the rest of the sugar and beat until thick and shiny. Carefully fold in the coconut mixture, being careful to retain as much air as possible.

5. Divide the mixture between the ramekins and level the tops with a palette knife. Run the tip of your thumb round the inside of the dish to create a lip as this will help the soufflés to rise evenly.

6. Transfer the ramekins to a roasting tin and pour just enough boiling water around them to come halfway up the sides. Bake 15–20 minutes or until they are well risen and a pale golden brown. Dust with icing sugar and serve immediately.

TOP TIP

Drizzle each soufflé with a little coconut rum for an adults-only treat.

Chocolate Tart

RVES 8

EPARATION TIME 35 MINUTES

OKING TIME 35 MINUTES

GREDIENTS

5 g / 8 oz / 2 ¼ cups ground almonds
5 g / 8 oz / 1 cup butter, softened
5 g / 8 oz / 1 cup caster (superfine) sugar
arge eggs
osp unsweetened cocoa powder, plus extra
for dusting
g / 2 ½ oz / ½ cup milk chocolate, grated
osp plain (all-purpose) flour
ng (confectioners') sugar for dusting

r the pastry

0 g / 3 ½ oz / ½ cup butter, cubed and chilled
0 g / 7 oz / 1 ⅓ cups plain (all-purpose) flour
gg, beaten
osp caster (superfine) sugar

METHOD

1. First make the pastry. Rub the butter into the flour until the mixture resembles fine breadcrumbs. Stir in just enough cold water to bring the pastry together into a pliable dough then chill for 30 minutes.

2. Preheat the oven to 200°C (180°C fan) / 390F / gas 6.

3. Roll out the pastry on a floured surface and use it to line a 23 cm (9 in) round tart case. Prick the pastry with a fork, line with cling film and fill with baking beans or rice. Bake for 10 minutes then remove the cling film and baking beans.

4. Whisk together the almonds, butter, sugar, eggs, cocoa, chocolate and flour until well whipped and smooth, then spoon the mixture into the pastry case.

5. Bake the tart for 25 minutes or until the filling is cooked through and the pastry is crisp underneath. Dust the tart with a little cocoa and icing sugar and serve hot or cold.

TOP TIP
Try serving the tart with orange sorbet for a refreshing accompaniment.

Jam Tarts with Spiced Pastry

MAKES 6

PREPARATION TIME 1 HOUR

COOKING TIME 25 MINUTES

INGREDIENTS

225 g / 8 oz / 1 ½ cups plain (all-purpose) flour
2 tsp mixed spice
110 g / 4 oz / ½ cup butter, cubed and chilled
250 ml / 9 fl. oz / 1 cup strawberry jam (jelly)
1 egg, beaten

METHOD

1. Preheat the oven to 200°C (180°C fan) / 400F / gas 6.

2. Sieve the flour and spice into a mixing bowl, then rub in the butter until the mixture resembles fine breadcrumbs. Stir in just enough cold water to bring the pastry together into a pliable dough. Chill for 30 minutes.

3. Roll out the pastry on a floured surface and cut out 6 circles, then use them to line 6 tartlet tins. Re-roll the trimmings and cut the sheet into 1 cm (½ in) strips.

4. Spoon the jam into the pastry cases, then lay the pastry strips over the top in a lattice pattern and crimp the edges to seal. Brush the pastry with beaten egg.

5. Bake the tartlets for 25 minutes or until the pastry is cooked underneath and golden brown on top.

TOP TIP
Serve the tarts with a drizzle of pouring cream.

trawberry nd Chocolate Meringue Pie

RVES 8

EPARATION TIME **1 HOUR**

)KING TIME **28 MINUTES**

GREDIENTS

- g / 3 ½ oz / ½ cup butter, cubed
- g / 7 oz / 1 ⅓ cups plain (all-purpose) flour
- sp unsweetened cocoa powder
- sp strawberry jam (jelly)
- rge egg whites
- g / 3 ½ oz / ½ cup caster (superfine) sugar
- g / 5 ½ oz / 1 cup strawberries
- g (confectioners') sugar for dusting

METHOD

1. Preheat the oven to 200°C (180°C fan) / 390F / gas 6.

2. Rub the butter into the flour and cocoa, then add just enough cold water to bind. Chill for 30 minutes, then roll out on a floured surface. Use the pastry to line a 23 cm (9 in) loose-bottomed tart tin and prick it with a fork.

3. Line the pastry with cling film and fill with baking beans or rice, then bake for 10 minutes. Remove the cling film and beans and cook for another 8 minutes to crisp. Spoon the jam into the pastry case.

4. Whisk the egg whites until stiff, then gradually add the sugar and whisk until the mixture is thick and shiny. Spoon the meringue on top of the jam and smooth with a palette knife. Return to the oven for 10 minutes to lightly brown the top.

5. Leave to cool a little, then arrange the strawberries on top and dust with icing sugar.

TOP TIP

Try using raspberries instead of strawberries.

Apple and Date Filo Pies

METHOD

1. Preheat the oven to 200°C (180°C fan) / 400F / gas 6.

2. Put the apples, dates, sugar and spice in a saucepan with 4 tbsp of cold water. Put lid on the pan, then cook over a gentle heat for 10 minutes, stirring occasionally.

3. Taste the compote and add more sugar if necessary, then divide it between 6 mini casserole dishes.

4. Melt the butter, then brush it over each filo sheet, stacking them up as you go. Use a large round cookie cutter to cut out 6 circles, then crumple them slightly and lay on top of the casserole dishes.

5. Bake the pies for 10 minutes or until the filo is golden and crisp. Dust with icing sugar and serve immediately.

MAKES 6

PREPARATION TIME 20 MINUTES

COOKING TIME 20 MINUTES

INGREDIENTS

1 large cooking apple, peeled, cored and diced
3 eating apples, peeled, cored and diced
100 g / 3 ½ oz / ½ cup dates, stoned and chopped
2 tbsp light brown sugar
1 tsp mixed spice
100 g / 3 ½ oz / ½ cup butter
250 g / 9 oz / ¾ cup filo pastry sheets
icing (confectioners') sugar to dust

TOP TIP
Try replacing the dates with dried figs.

Lemon, Raspberry and Pistachio Cheesecake

RVES 8

EPARATION TIME **4 HOURS 40 MINUTES**

OKING TIME **4 HOURS**

GREDIENTS

g / 1 ¾ oz / ¼ cup butter

0 g / 7 oz / ¾ cup digestive biscuits, crushed

g / 1 ¾ oz / ½ cup pistachio nuts, chopped

g / 5 ½ oz / ⅔ cup cream cheese, well chilled

0 g / 5 ½ oz / ⅔ cup condensed milk, well chilled

emons, juiced

the topping

0 g / 1 ¾ oz / ½ cup raspberry jelly cubes

g / 1 ¾ oz / ½ cup pistachio nuts, chopped

METHOD

1. Melt the butter and stir in the crushed biscuits and chopped pistachio nuts, then tip the mixture into a 23 cm (9 in) round spring-form cake tin and press down firmly into an even layer.

2. Beat the cream cheese with an electric whisk until smooth, then whisk in the condensed milk. Whisk in the lemon juice until the mixture starts to thicken, then pour it onto the biscuit base and level the top. Chill in the fridge for 3 hours.

3. Make up the jelly according to the packet instructions, using half the recommended amount of water. Leave the jelly to cool a little, then flood the top of the cheesecake with it before it starts to set.

4. Return the cheesecake to the fridge for 1 hour. Un-mould the cheesecake and transfer it to a serving plate, then sprinkle with the chopped pistachios.

TOP TIP

Try replacing the pistachio nuts with walnuts.

Index

Strawberry Tartlets, 183
Summer Fruit Tartlets, 199

WALNUTS
Chocolate and Walnut Fondants, 207
Crusty Walnut Rolls, 52
Dundee Cake, 125
Toffee and Nut-topped Ginger
    Cake, 117
Wholemeal Walnut Loaf Cake, 110

WHISKY
Dundee Cake, 125

YEAST, EASY-BLEND DRIED
Baguettes, 48
Black Olive and Feta Bread, 27
Cheese and Bacon Bread, 43
Cheese Fougasse, 60
Cinnamon and Raisin Bread, 39
Crusty Lemon Rolls, 28
Crusty Walnut Rolls, 52
Floured Cob, 31
Giant Rum Baba, 121
Granary and Rye Batons, 16
Grape and Rosemary Focaccia, 32
Hazelnut and Fig Rolls, 63
Long-ferment Bread, 55
Onion Focaccia, 23
Rice Bread, 12
Rosemary Focaccia, 35
Rustic Focaccia, 59
Rye Bread, 44
Seeded White Rolls, 56
Seed-topped Square Rolls, 40
Seed-topped Wholemeal Rolls, 47
Sesame Rolls, 11
Sweetcorn Rolls, 24
Tear and Share Rolls, 36
White Bread Rolls, 20
Wholemeal Basil Bread, 8
Wholemeal Granary Batons, 51
Yogurt Bread, 15

YOGURT, NATURAL
Yogurt Bread, 15